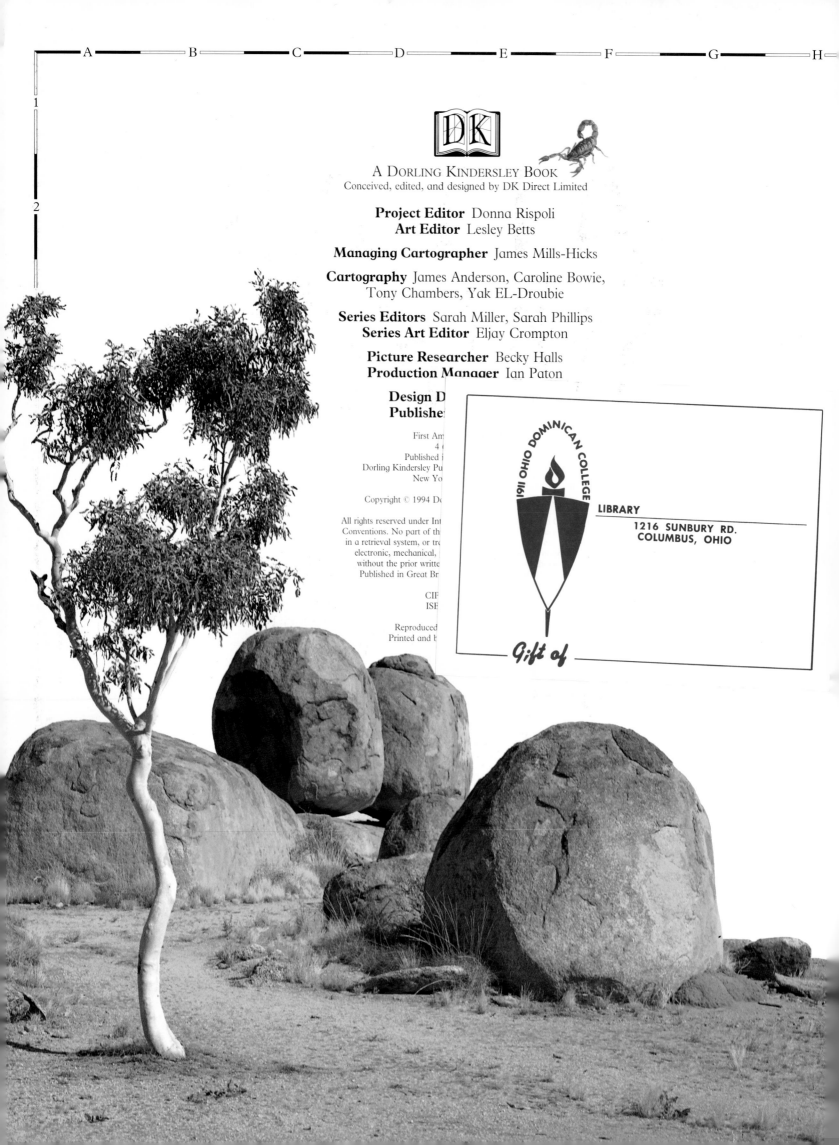

A DORLING KINDERSLEY BOOK
Conceived, edited, and designed by DK Direct Limited

Project Editor Donna Rispoli
Art Editor Lesley Betts

Managing Cartographer James Mills-Hicks

Cartography James Anderson, Caroline Bowie,
Tony Chambers, Yak EL-Droubie

Series Editors Sarah Miller, Sarah Phillips
Series Art Editor Eljay Crompton

Picture Researcher Becky Halls
Production Manager Ian Paton

Design D
Publishe

First Am
4 6
Published i
Dorling Kindersley Pu
New Yo

Copyright © 1994 Do

All rights reserved under Int
Conventions. No part of th
in a retrieval system, or tra
electronic, mechanical,
without the prior writte
Published in Great Br

CIP
ISB

Reproduced
Printed and b

ATLAS
OF THE
WORLD

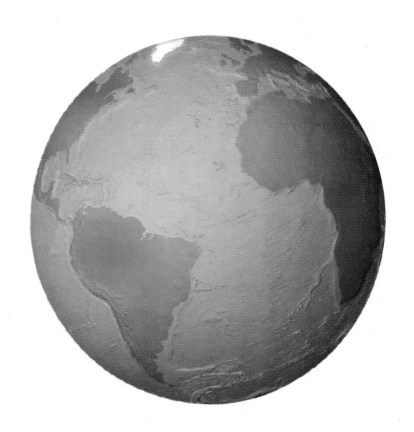

DORLING KINDERSLEY

LONDON • NEW YORK
STUTTGART

CONTENTS

HOW TO USE THIS ATLAS

Each map is colored, full of place names, and packed with different symbols, such as red dots and blue lines. The two keys on this page will help you work out what these colors and symbols mean. You can also learn how to use the index at the back of the book to find places on the maps.

Interesting natural regions, such as deserts and plateaus, are named on the map.

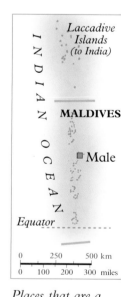

WHAT THE COLORS MEAN

Snow and ice

Tundra

Coniferous forest

Temperate forest

Temperate rain forest

Mediterranean vegetation

Temperate grassland

Cold desert

Hot desert

Tropical forest

Tropical rain forest

Tropical grassland

Mountains

Wetland

Places that are a long way from the mainland are put in a separate box.

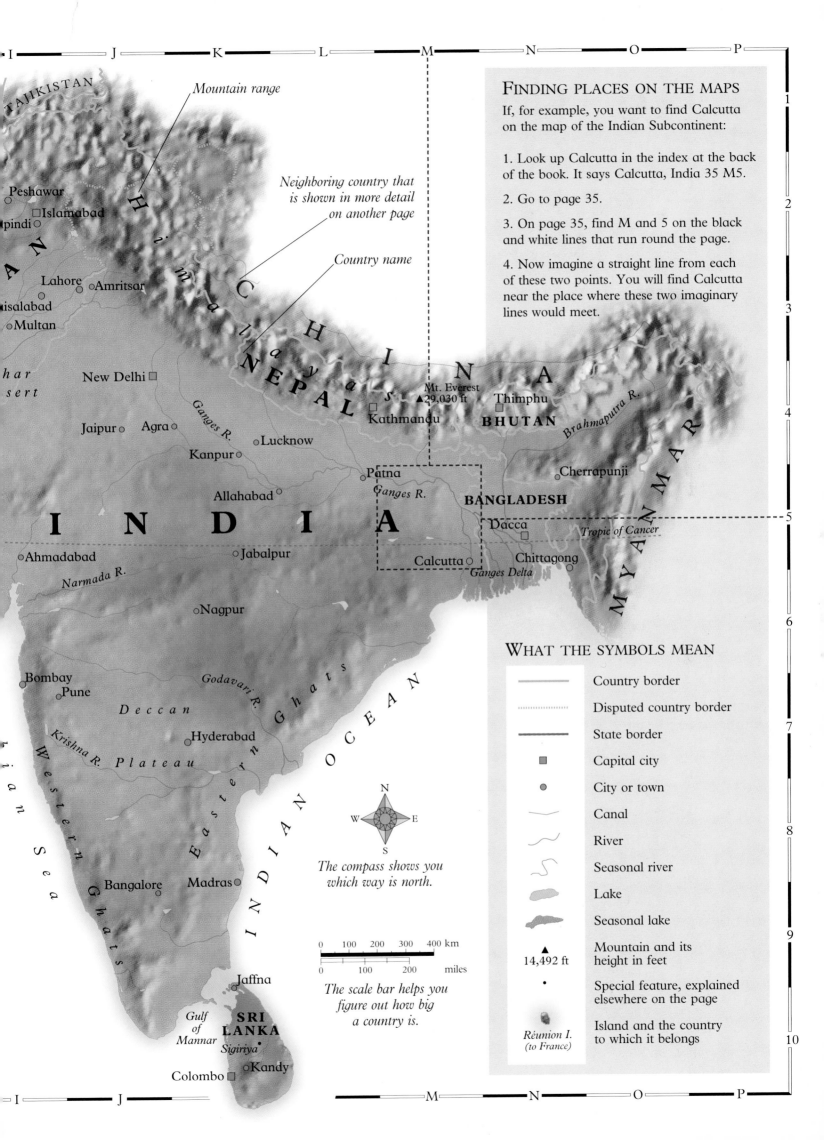

TAJIKISTAN

Mountain range

Peshawar

□ Islamabad

pindi

Lahore　Amritsar

isalabad

Multan

Neighboring country that is shown in more detail on another page

Country name

HIMALAYA

CHINA

NEPAL

har sert

New Delhi □

Jaipur　Agra

Ganges R.

Lucknow

Kanpur

Mt. Everest
▲29,030 ft

Kathmandu

Thimphu

BHUTAN

Brahmaputra R.

MYANMAR

Cherrapunji

Patna

Ganges R.

Allahabad

BANGLADESH

INDIA

Dacca □

Tropic of Cancer

Ahmadabad

Jabalpur

Calcutta

Chittagong

Narmada R.

Ganges Delta

Nagpur

Bombay

Pune

Godavari R.

Deccan

Krishna R.　*Plateau*

Hyderabad

Eastern Ghats

Western Ghats

INDIAN OCEAN

ian Sea

Bangalore

Madras

Jaffna

*Gulf
of
Mannar*

SRI
LANKA

Sigiriya

Colombo □　Kandy

FINDING PLACES ON THE MAPS

If, for example, you want to find Calcutta on the map of the Indian Subcontinent:

1. Look up Calcutta in the index at the back of the book. It says Calcutta, India 35 M5.

2. Go to page 35.

3. On page 35, find M and 5 on the black and white lines that run round the page.

4. Now imagine a straight line from each of these two points. You will find Calcutta near the place where these two imaginary lines would meet.

N
W　　E
S

The compass shows you which way is north.

0　100　200　300　400 km
0　　100　　200　miles

The scale bar helps you figure out how big a country is.

WHAT THE SYMBOLS MEAN

───────	Country border
···········	Disputed country border
───────	State border
■	Capital city
●	City or town
～	Canal
～	River
～	Seasonal river
▬	Lake
▬	Seasonal lake
▲ 14,492 ft	Mountain and its height in feet
•	Special feature, explained elsewhere on the page
🗻 *Réunion I. (to France)*	Island and the country to which it belongs

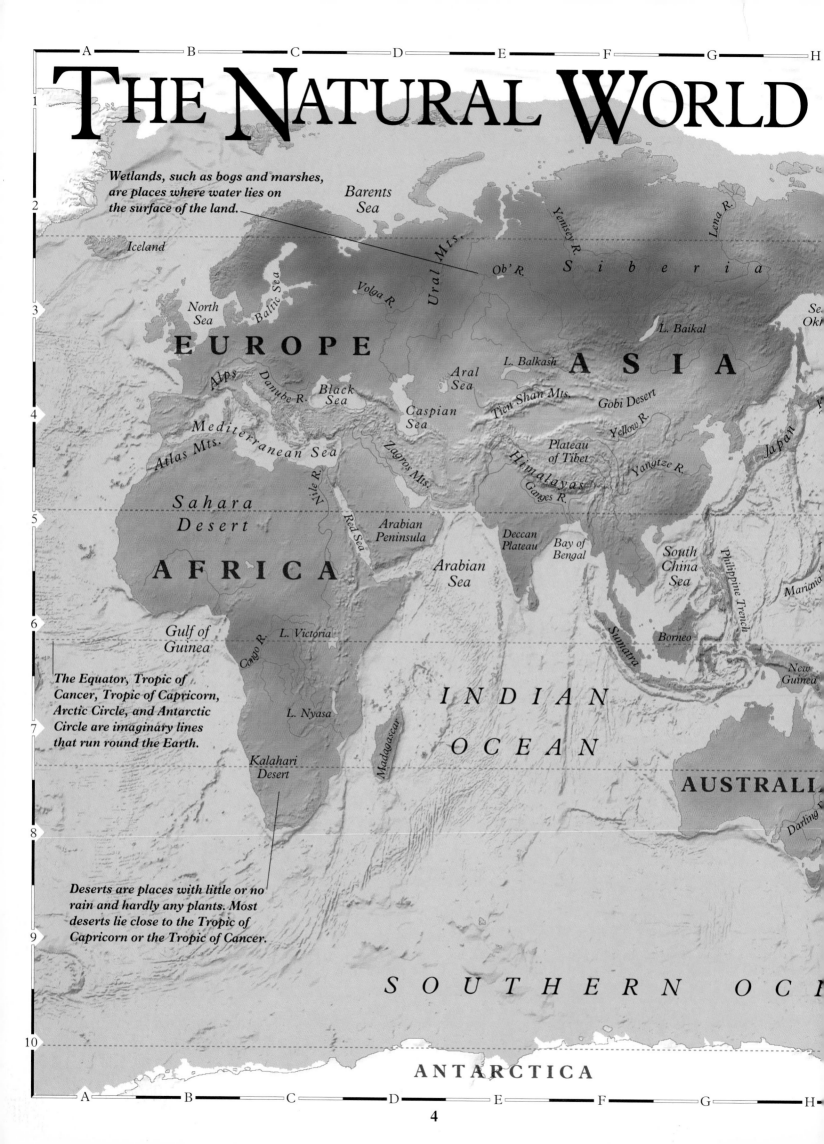

THE NATURAL WORLD

Wetlands, such as bogs and marshes, are places where water lies on the surface of the land.

Barents Sea

Iceland

Ural Mts.

Ob' R.

Yenisey R.

Lena R.

S i b e r i a

Se. Okl.

North Sea

Baltic Sea

Volga R.

L. Baikal

EUROPE

ASIA

Alps

Danube R.

Black Sea

Caspian Sea

Aral Sea

L. Balkash

Tien Shan Mts.

Gobi Desert

Mediterranean Sea

Atlas Mts.

Zagros Mts.

Nile R.

Yellow R.

Plateau of Tibet

Himalayas

Yangtze R.

Japan

Sahara Desert

Red Sea

Arabian Peninsula

Ganges R.

Deccan Plateau

Bay of Bengal

South China Sea

Philippine Trench

Mariana

AFRICA

Arabian Sea

Gulf of Guinea

Congo R.

L. Victoria

Sumatra

Borneo

New Guinea

The Equator, Tropic of Cancer, Tropic of Capricorn, Arctic Circle, and Antarctic Circle are imaginary lines that run round the Earth.

L. Nyasa

Madagascar

I N D I A N

O C E A N

Kalahari Desert

AUSTRALIA

Darling

Deserts are places with little or no rain and hardly any plants. Most deserts lie close to the Tropic of Capricorn or the Tropic of Cancer.

S O U T H E R N   O C E

ANTARCTICA

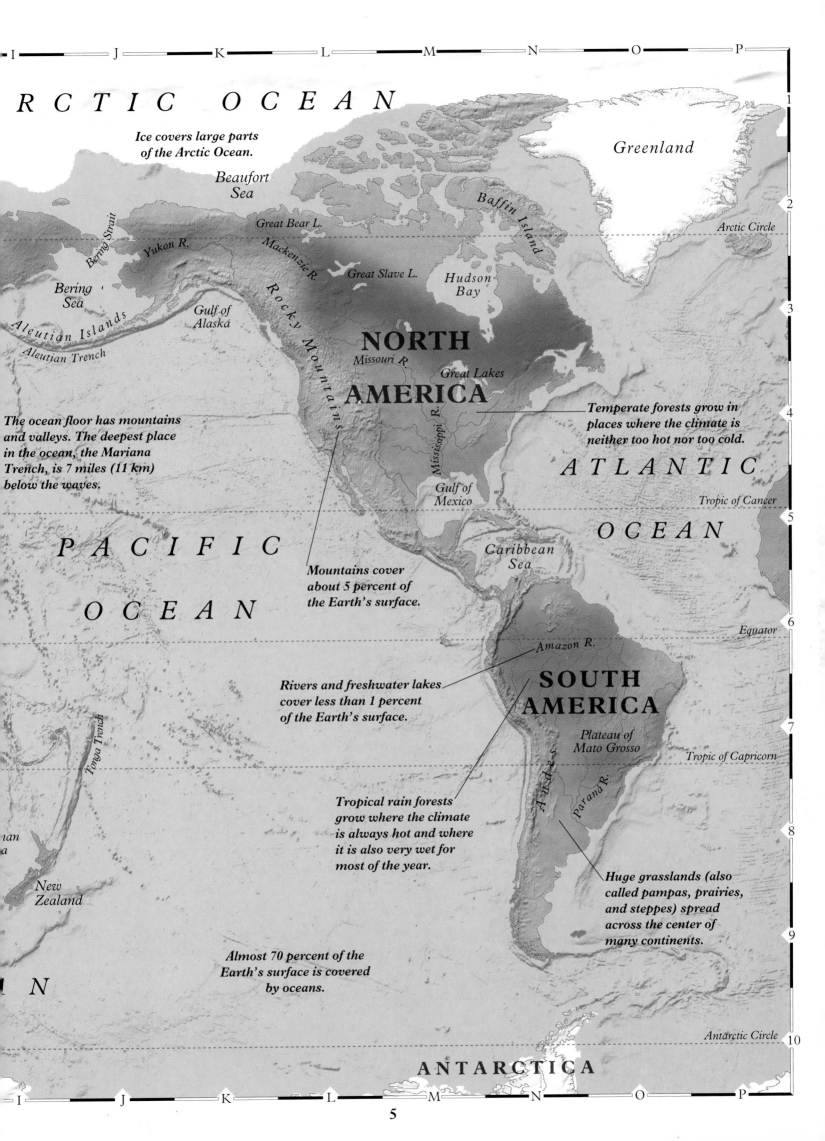

ARCTIC OCEAN

Ice covers large parts
of the Arctic Ocean.

Greenland

*Beaufort
Sea*

Baffin Island

Arctic Circle

Great Bear L.

Bering Strait

Yukon R.

Mackenzie R.

Great Slave L.

*Hudson
Bay*

*Bering
Sea*

Aleutian Islands

*Gulf of
Alaska*

Aleutian Trench

Rocky Mountains

**NORTH
AMERICA**

Missouri R.

Great Lakes

The ocean floor has mountains
and valleys. The deepest place
in the ocean, the Mariana
Trench, is 7 miles (11 km)
below the waves.

Temperate forests grow in
places where the climate is
neither too hot nor too cold.

ATLANTIC

Mississippi R.

*Gulf of
Mexico*

Tropic of Cancer

PACIFIC

OCEAN

Mountains cover
about 5 percent of
the Earth's surface.

*Caribbean
Sea*

OCEAN

Amazon R.

Equator

Rivers and freshwater lakes
cover less than 1 percent
of the Earth's surface.

**SOUTH
AMERICA**

*Plateau of
Mato Grosso*

Tonga Trench

Tropic of Capricorn

Tropical rain forests
grow where the climate
is always hot and where
it is also very wet for
most of the year.

Andes

Paraná R.

*New
Zealand*

Huge grasslands (also
called pampas, prairies,
and steppes) spread
across the center of
many continents.

Almost 70 percent of the
Earth's surface is covered
by oceans.

Antarctic Circle

ANTARCTICA

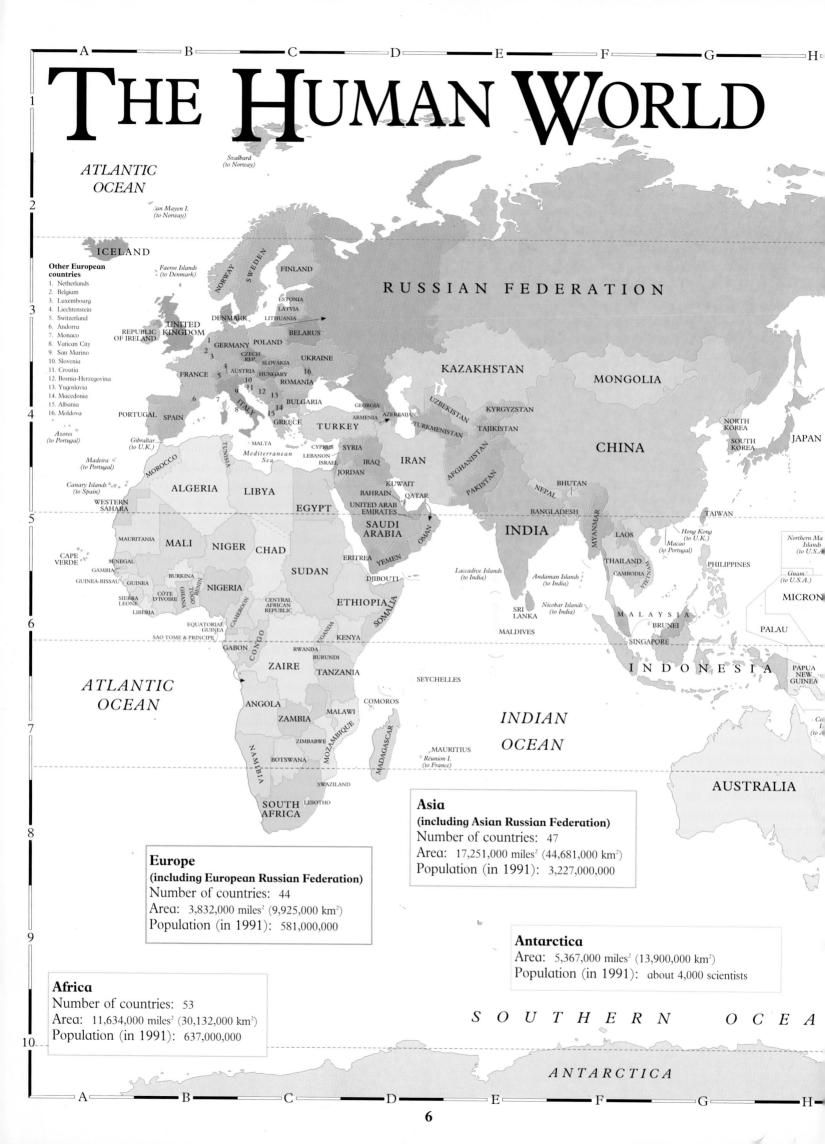

THE HUMAN WORLD

ATLANTIC OCEAN

Svalbard (to Norway)

ICELAND

San Mayen I. (to Norway)

Other European countries
1. Netherlands
2. Belgium
3. Luxembourg
4. Liechtenstein
5. Switzerland
6. Andorra
7. Monaco
8. Vatican City
9. San Marino
10. Slovenia
11. Croatia
12. Bosnia-Herzegovina
13. Yugoslavia
14. Macedonia
15. Albania
16. Moldova

Faeroe Islands (to Denmark)

NORWAY
SWEDEN
FINLAND

RUSSIAN FEDERATION

ESTONIA
LATVIA
LITHUANIA

DENMARK

REPUBLIC OF IRELAND
UNITED KINGDOM

GERMANY
POLAND
BELARUS

CZECH REP.
SLOVAKIA
UKRAINE

FRANCE
AUSTRIA
HUNGARY
ROMANIA

ITALY
BULGARIA
GREECE

KAZAKHSTAN

MONGOLIA

PORTUGAL
SPAIN

GEORGIA
ARMENIA
AZERBAIJAN
TURKEY

UZBEKISTAN
KYRGYZSTAN
TURKMENISTAN
TAJIKISTAN

CHINA

NORTH KOREA
SOUTH KOREA
JAPAN

Azores (to Portugal)

Madeira (to Portugal)

Gibraltar (to U.K.)
MALTA
Mediterranean Sea
CYPRUS
SYRIA
LEBANON
ISRAEL
IRAQ
IRAN
AFGHANISTAN
PAKISTAN
NEPAL
BHUTAN

Canary Islands (to Spain)

MOROCCO
TUNISIA

WESTERN SAHARA

ALGERIA
LIBYA
EGYPT
JORDAN
KUWAIT
BAHRAIN
QATAR
UNITED ARAB EMIRATES
SAUDI ARABIA
OMAN

BANGLADESH
INDIA
MYANMAR
LAOS
TAIWAN

Hong Kong (to U.K.)
Macao (to Portugal)

Northern Ma... Islands (to U.S.A.)

MAURITANIA
MALI
NIGER
CHAD

CAPE VERDE

SENEGAL
GAMBIA
GUINEA-BISSAU
GUINEA
SIERRA LEONE
LIBERIA
BURKINA
CÔTE D'IVOIRE
GHANA
TOGO
BENIN
NIGERIA
CAMEROON
CENTRAL AFRICAN REPUBLIC

SUDAN
ERITREA
DJIBOUTI
YEMEN
ETHIOPIA
SOMALIA

Laccadive Islands (to India)

Andaman Islands (to India)

THAILAND
CAMBODIA
PHILIPPINES

Guam (to U.S.A.)

MICRON...

EQUATORIAL GUINEA
SAO TOME & PRINCIPE
GABON
CONGO
ZAIRE

UGANDA
KENYA
RWANDA
BURUNDI
TANZANIA

SRI LANKA
MALDIVES

Nicobar Islands (to India)

MALAYSIA
BRUNEI
SINGAPORE

PALAU

SEYCHELLES

INDONESIA

PAPUA NEW GUINEA

ATLANTIC OCEAN

ANGOLA
ZAMBIA
MALAWI
COMOROS

INDIAN OCEAN

ZIMBABWE
MOZAMBIQUE
NAMIBIA
BOTSWANA
MADAGASCAR

MAURITIUS
Réunion I. (to France)

Co... L... (to A...)

SWAZILAND
SOUTH AFRICA
LESOTHO

AUSTRALIA

Asia
(including Asian Russian Federation)
Number of countries: 47
Area: 17,251,000 miles^2 (44,681,000 km^2)
Population (in 1991): 3,227,000,000

Europe
(including European Russian Federation)
Number of countries: 44
Area: 3,832,000 miles^2 (9,925,000 km^2)
Population (in 1991): 581,000,000

Antarctica
Area: 5,367,000 miles^2 (13,900,000 km^2)
Population (in 1991): about 4,000 scientists

Africa
Number of countries: 53
Area: 11,634,000 miles^2 (30,132,000 km^2)
Population (in 1991): 637,000,000

SOUTHERN OCEA...

ANTARCTICA

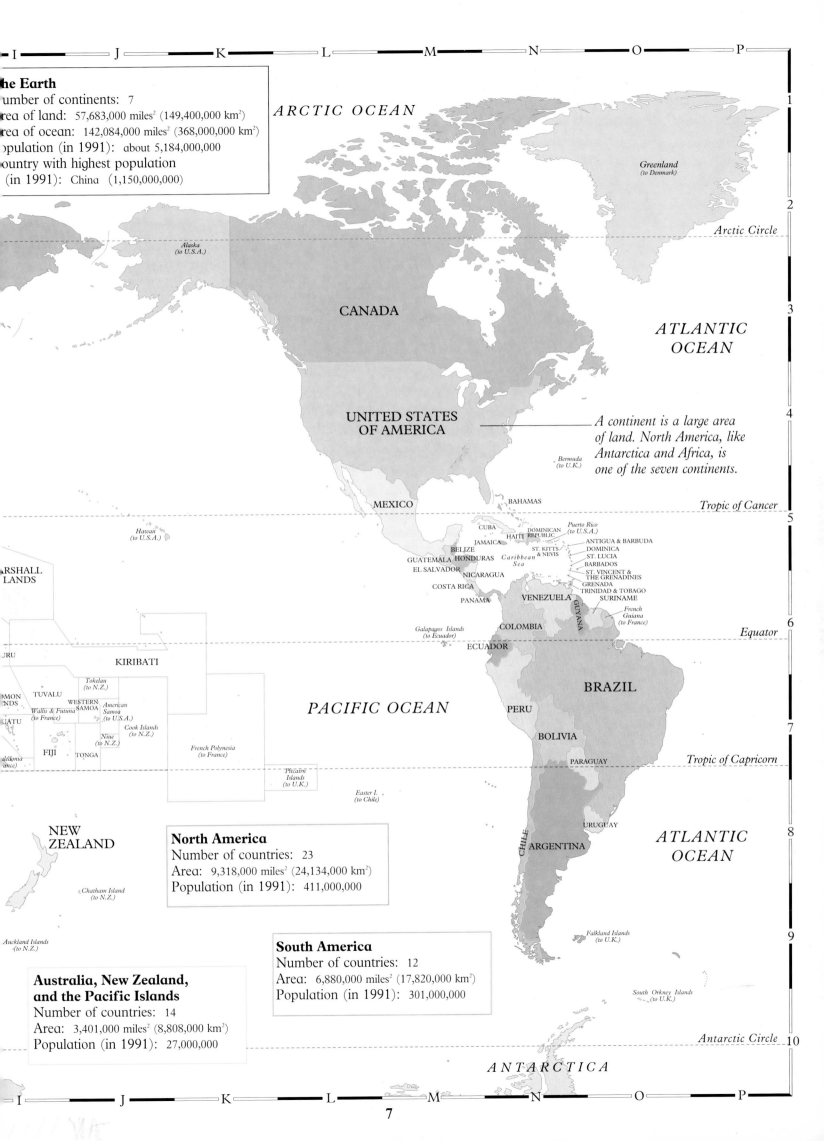

The Earth
Number of continents: 7
Area of land: 57,683,000 miles² (149,400,000 km²)
Area of ocean: 142,084,000 miles² (368,000,000 km²)
Population (in 1991): about 5,184,000,000
Country with highest population
(in 1991): China (1,150,000,000)

ARCTIC OCEAN

Greenland
(to Denmark)

Arctic Circle

Alaska
(to U.S.A.)

CANADA

*ATLANTIC
OCEAN*

UNITED STATES
OF AMERICA

Bermuda
(to U.K.)

*A continent is a large area
of land. North America, like
Antarctica and Africa, is
one of the seven continents.*

MEXICO

BAHAMAS

Tropic of Cancer

Hawaii
(to U.S.A.)

CUBA
JAMAICA
BELIZE
GUATEMALA HONDURAS
EL SALVADOR
NICARAGUA
COSTA RICA
PANAMA

DOMINICAN
REPUBLIC
HAITI

Puerto Rico
(to U.S.A.)

ANTIGUA & BARBUDA
DOMINICA
ST. LUCIA
BARBADOS
ST. VINCENT &
THE GRENADINES
GRENADA
TRINIDAD & TOBAGO
SURINAME

ST. KITTS
& NEVIS

*Caribbean
Sea*

MARSHALL
ISLANDS

Galapagos Islands
(to Ecuador)

VENEZUELA

GUYANA

French
Guiana
(to France)

COLOMBIA

Equator

NAURU

KIRIBATI

ECUADOR

BRAZIL

TUVALU
SOLOMON
ISLANDS
VANUATU

Tokelau
(to N.Z.)

WESTERN
SAMOA
Wallis & Futuna
(to France)

American
Samoa
(to U.S.A.)

Cook Islands
(to N.Z.)

Niue
(to N.Z.)

PACIFIC OCEAN

PERU

BOLIVIA

New
Caledonia
(France)

FIJI

TONGA

French Polynesia
(to France)

Pitcairn
Islands
(to U.K.)

Easter I.
(to Chile)

PARAGUAY

Tropic of Capricorn

NEW
ZEALAND

Chatham Island
(to N.Z.)

North America
Number of countries: 23
Area: 9,318,000 miles² (24,134,000 km²)
Population (in 1991): 411,000,000

URUGUAY

CHILE
ARGENTINA

*ATLANTIC
OCEAN*

Auckland Islands
(to N.Z.)

South America
Number of countries: 12
Area: 6,880,000 miles² (17,820,000 km²)
Population (in 1991): 301,000,000

Falkland Islands
(to U.K.)

**Australia, New Zealand,
and the Pacific Islands**
Number of countries: 14
Area: 3,401,000 miles² (8,808,000 km²)
Population (in 1991): 27,000,000

South Orkney Islands
(to U.K.)

Antarctic Circle

ANTARCTICA

THE ARCTIC & ANTARCTICA

The areas around the North and South Poles, which lie on opposite sides of the planet, are covered in ice. Although they look alike, these areas are different. The Arctic, in the north, is a frozen ocean surrounded by land. Antarctica, however, is a vast area of land surrounded by an ocean. This southern, frozen area is almost twice the size of Australia. It is one of Earth's great landmasses, or continents.

Icy Marvel
Icebergs are pieces of floating ice. This iceberg is off Cape Farvel in Greenland. It looks big, but you can't see how huge it really is because 90 percent of it is underwater.

Greenland is an enormous island. It is four times larger than France.

The Arctic Ocean is the smallest of the Earth's oceans

Arctic Circle
Bering Strait
ALASKA (to U.S.A.)
Wrangel I.
RUSSIAN FEDERATION
Beaufort Sea
Limit of Permanent Pack Ice
New Siberian Islands
Banks I.
Laptev Sea
A R C T I C
Queen Elizabeth Islands
O C E A N
Severnaya Zemlya
Limit of Permanent Pack Ice
North Pole
Kara Sea
CANADA
Ellesmere I.
Thule
Franz Josef Land
Baffin I.
Baffin Bay
Barents Sea
Svalbard (to Norway)
Longyearbyen
Davis Strait
Greenland (to Denmark)
Greenland Sea
Godthâb
Arctic Circle
Denmark Strait
Cape Farvel
ATLANTIC OCEAN

0 200 400 600 800 1000 km
0 200 400 600 miles

Green Summer
Low-growing tundra plants brighten up the coastal edges of icy Greenland. Grasses, mosses, and lichen carpet these areas.

Pack of Ice
In July, during Antarctica's winter, the seas around the mountainous Antarctic Peninsula can freeze as far as 1,240 miles (2,000 km) from the land. This frozen sea is called pack ice.

The Ice Life
Many of the animals that live in these freezing lands have a thick layer of fat under their skin to protect them from the bitter cold.

Arctic Animals

Polar bear

200   400   600   800   1000 km

200   400   600   miles

The Weddell Sea is full of life. Huge blue whales feed on tiny creatures, called krill.

Walrus

The lowest temperature ever recorded on Earth was at Vostok. It fell to -128.6°F (-89.2°C).

Antarctic Animals

Mount Erebus is a volcano. It sometimes throws out pieces of boiling lava onto the snow.

SOUTHERN OCEAN

South Orkney Islands (to U.K.)

South Shetland Islands (to U.K.)

Anvers I.

Antarctic Circle

Weddell Sea

Antarctic Peninsula

Bellingshausen Sea

Peter 1st I. (to Norway)

Amundsen Sea

Marie Byrd Land

Ronne Ice Shelf

Ellsworth Mts.

Transantarctic Mountains

Queen Maud Land

ANTARCTICA

SOUTH POLAR PLATEAU

South Pole
Amundsen-Scott (Research Station)

Enderby Land

Antarctic Circle

Lambert Glacier

Davis Sea

Vostok (Research Station)

Ross Ice Shelf

Scott Base (Research Station)

Mt. Erebus 12,448 ft

Ross Sea

Cape Adare

Victoria Land

Wilkes Land

SOUTHERN OCEAN

An ice sheet is made of snow that fell millions of years ago.

Emperor penguin

Blue whale

Sea Shelf
In winter, the thick layer of ice that covers Antarctica spreads so much, it spills onto the sea to form a shelf of floating ice. The Ross Ice Shelf is as high as the Eiffel Tower.

CANADA

The enormous country sandwiched between the United States and the Arctic is called Canada. Thousands of years ago, much of this land was covered by ice, which carved out features such as the Great Lakes – the largest system of lakes on Earth. Today the climate is warmer, and forests and grasslands spread over much of Canada. Ice still covers many of the islands in the far north.

Coast to Coast
The conifer trees growing by this lake in Alberta are part of an enormous forest that stretches across Canada. These tough trees can cope with a wide range of climates, from freezing cold winters to hot summers.

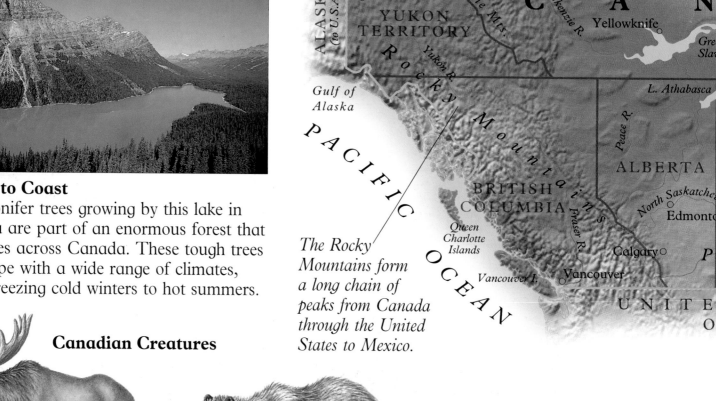

The Rocky Mountains form a long chain of peaks from Canada through the United States to Mexico.

Canadian Creatures

Moose

Grizzly bear

Timber wolf

North American porcupine

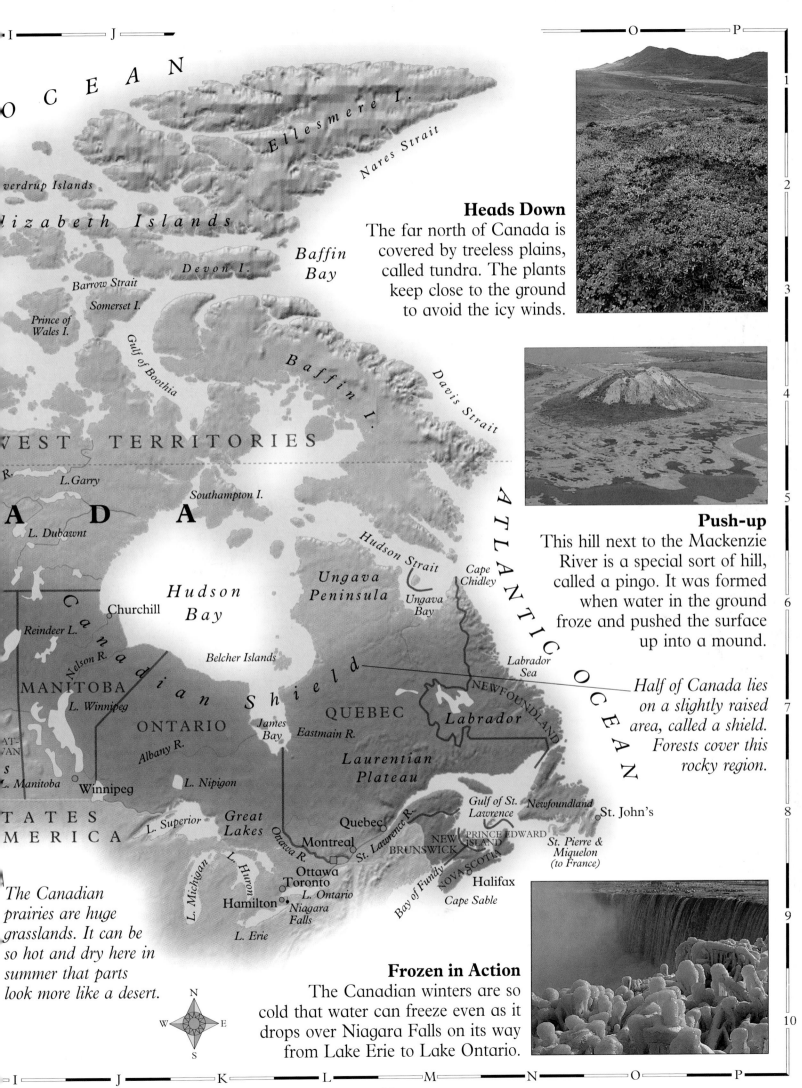

O C E A N

verdrup Islands

Ellesmere I.

lizabeth Islands

Devon I.

Baffin Bay

Nares Strait

Barrow Strait

Somerset I.

Prince of Wales I.

Gulf of Boothia

Baffin I.

Davis Strait

Heads Down
The far north of Canada is covered by treeless plains, called tundra. The plants keep close to the ground to avoid the icy winds.

WEST T E R R I T O R I E S

R.

L. Garry

Southampton I.

A D A

L. Dubawnt

Hudson Strait

Ungava Peninsula

Cape Chidley

Ungava Bay

A T L A N T I C O C E A N

Push-up
This hill next to the Mackenzie River is a special sort of hill, called a pingo. It was formed when water in the ground froze and pushed the surface up into a mound.

Hudson Bay

Churchill

Reindeer L.

Belcher Islands

Labrador Sea

Canadian Shield

Nelson R.

MANITOBA

L. Winnipeg

ONTARIO

James Bay

QUEBEC

Labrador

NEWFOUNDLAND

Half of Canada lies on a slightly raised area, called a shield. Forests cover this rocky region.

AT-VAN

s

L. Manitoba

Winnipeg

Albany R.

Eastmain R.

Laurentian Plateau

TATES

MERICA

L. Superior

Great Lakes

L. Nipigon

Ottawa R.

St. Lawrence R.

Quebec

Montreal

Gulf of St. Lawrence

Newfoundland

St. John's

NEW BRUNSWICK

PRINCE EDWARD ISLAND

St. Pierre & Miquelon (to France)

L. Michigan

L. Huron

Ottawa

Toronto

L. Ontario

Hamilton

Niagara Falls

St. Lawrence R.

NOVA SCOTIA

Bay of Fundy

Halifax

Cape Sable

L. Erie

The Canadian prairies are huge grasslands. It can be so hot and dry here in summer that parts look more like a desert.

N
W   E
S

Frozen in Action
The Canadian winters are so cold that water can freeze even as it drops over Niagara Falls on its way from Lake Erie to Lake Ontario.

THE UNITED STATES

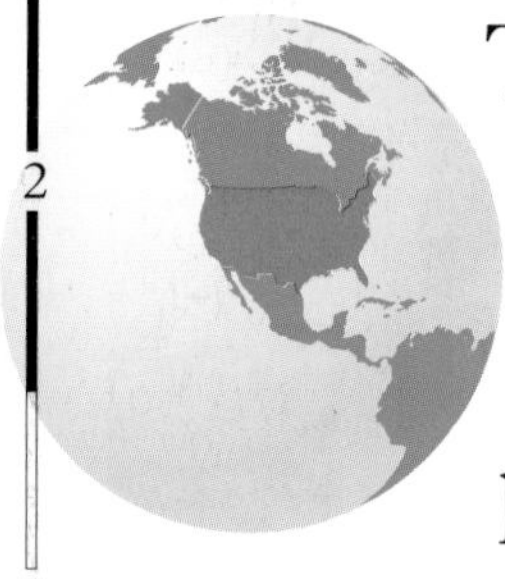

The climate in the United States is very varied – Alaska in the far north is icy cold, yet Florida in the south is tropical. However, most of this region has a milder climate. The vast open spaces in the middle of this massive country are filled by grasslands, called the prairies and Great Plains. In the west, the land rises up to form the mighty Rocky Mountains. The huge, hot deserts in the southwest of the country contrast with the cool, temperate forests along the eastern coast.

Beaver

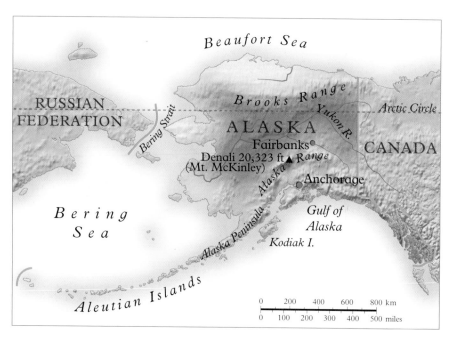

Beaufort Sea

RUSSIAN FEDERATION

Bering Strait

Brooks Range

ALASKA

Yukon R.

Arctic Circle

CANADA

Fairbanks
Denali 20,323 ft ▲ Range
(Mt. McKinley)

Alaska

Anchorage

Bering Sea

Gulf of Alaska

Kodiak I.

Alaska Peninsula

Aleutian Islands

0	200	400	600	800 km
0	100	200	300	400	500 miles

The United States is made up of 50 states. Two of these, Alaska and Hawaii, are separated from the rest. Alaska lies next to northwest Canada. Hawaii lies 2,300 miles (3,700 km) off the west coast of the mainland United States.

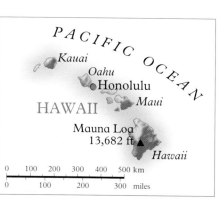

PACIFIC OCEAN

Kauai

Oahu
Honolulu

Maui

HAWAII

Mauna Loa
13,682 ft ▲

Hawaii

0	100	200	300	400	500 km
0	100	200	300 miles

High and Dry
Flat-topped towers of rock, called buttes, stand on the hot desert floor of Monument Valley. They are the remains of a large plateau that has been worn away.

(Map labels: WASHINGTON, Seattle, Mt. St. Helens 8,367 ft, Portland, Columbia R., Cascade Range, Coast Range, OREGON, Snake R., IDAHO, Boise, Rocky Mountains, L. For..., Helena, MONTANA, WY..., Great Salt L., Great Basin, Salt Lake City, Carson City, Pyramid L., San Francisco, Sierra Nevada, CALIFORNIA, NEVADA, UN..., UTAH, Monument Valley, Death Valley, Mt. Whitney 14,492 ft, San Andreas Fault, Los Angeles, Salton Sea, Colorado R., Grand Canyon, ARIZONA, Phoenix, San Diego, Sonoran Desert, PACIFIC OCEAN, CA...)

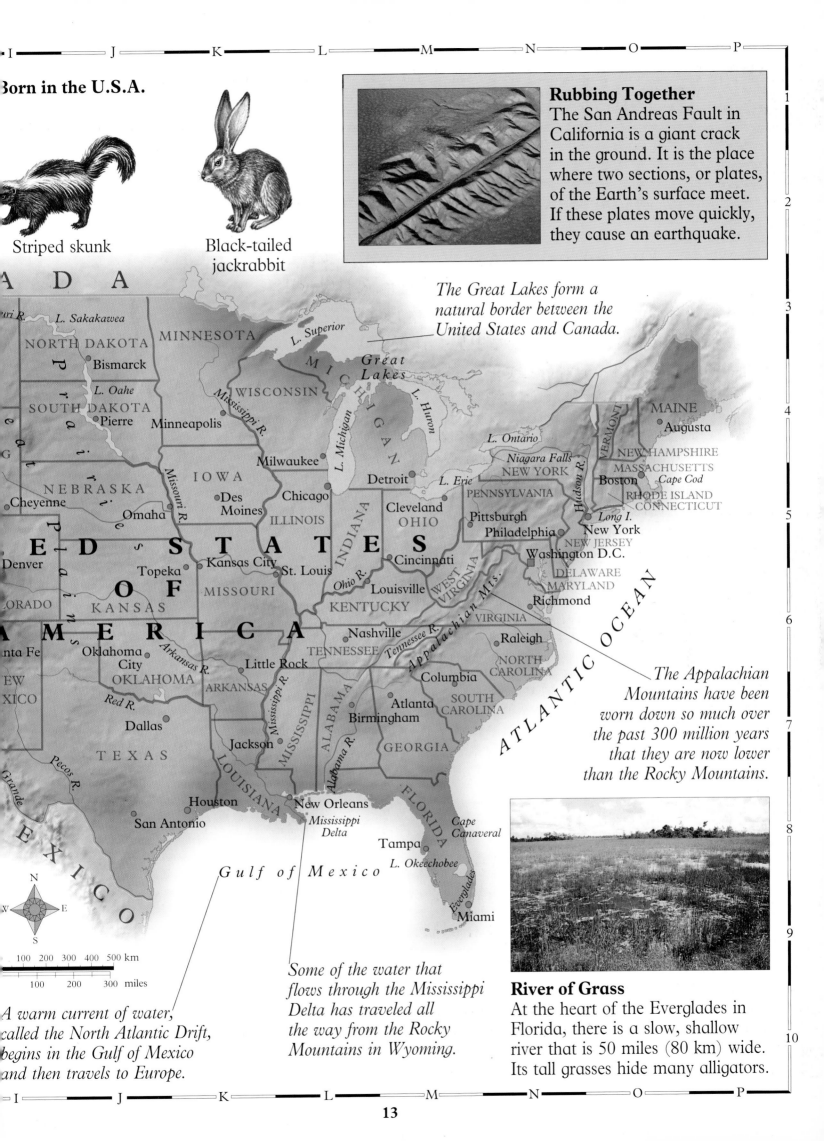

Born in the U.S.A.

Striped skunk

Black-tailed
jackrabbit

Rubbing Together
The San Andreas Fault in
California is a giant crack
in the ground. It is the place
where two sections, or plates,
of the Earth's surface meet.
If these plates move quickly,
they cause an earthquake.

The Great Lakes form a
natural border between the
United States and Canada.

CANADA

Missouri R.
L. Sakakawea

NORTH DAKOTA
Bismarck

MINNESOTA

L. Superior

MICHIGAN

Great
Lakes

L. Huron

MAINE
Augusta

L. Oahe

SOUTH DAKOTA
Pierre

WISCONSIN

Mississippi R.

L. Michigan

VERMONT

NEW HAMPSHIRE

Minneapolis

L. Ontario

Niagara Falls

MASSACHUSETTS

Prairie

Milwaukee

NEW YORK

Hudson R.

Boston

Cape Cod

NEBRASKA

IOWA

Detroit

Cleveland

L. Erie

PENNSYLVANIA

Pittsburgh

RHODE ISLAND
CONNECTICUT

Long I.

Cheyenne

Des
Moines

Chicago

OHIO

Philadelphia

New York

Omaha

Missouri R.

ILLINOIS

INDIANA

Cincinnati

NEW JERSEY

Denver

UNITED STATES

Kansas City

St. Louis

Washington D.C.

DELAWARE

Topeka

MARYLAND

OF

Ohio R.

Louisville

WEST
VIRGINIA

Richmond

COLORADO

KANSAS

MISSOURI

KENTUCKY

VIRGINIA

AMERICA

Nashville

Tennessee R.

Appalachian Mts.

Raleigh

Santa Fe

Oklahoma
City

Arkansas R.

TENNESSEE

NORTH
CAROLINA

NEW
MEXICO

OKLAHOMA

Little Rock

Columbia

Great Plains

ARKANSAS

Mississippi R.

Atlanta

SOUTH
CAROLINA

Red R.

ALABAMA

Birmingham

ATLANTIC OCEAN

Dallas

Jackson

MISSISSIPPI

Alabama R.

GEORGIA

TEXAS

Pecos R.

LOUISIANA

FLORIDA

Houston

New Orleans

Cape
Canaveral

San Antonio

Mississippi
Delta

Tampa

Rio Grande

L. Okeechobee

Gulf of Mexico

Everglades

MEXICO

Miami

N
W   E
S

100 200 300 400 500 km

100   200   300 miles

The Appalachian
Mountains have been
worn down so much over
the past 300 million years
that they are now lower
than the Rocky Mountains.

River of Grass
At the heart of the Everglades in
Florida, there is a slow, shallow
river that is 50 miles (80 km) wide.
Its tall grasses hide many alligators.

A warm current of water,
called the North Atlantic Drift,
begins in the Gulf of Mexico
and then travels to Europe.

Some of the water that
flows through the Mississippi
Delta has traveled all
the way from the Rocky
Mountains in Wyoming.

CENTRAL AMERICA & THE CARIBBEAN

The narrow strip of land connecting the United States to South America is known as Central America. All the way along this land bridge, there are chains of mountains and active volcanoes. In the north, there are cool, high plateaus and hot, dry deserts. It is wet enough farther south for tropical rain forests. The warm Caribbean waters that wash the southeast coast of this region contain two groups of tropical islands, the Greater and Lesser Antilles, often called the Caribbean islands.

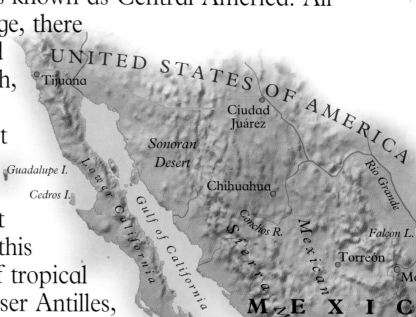

UNITED STATES OF AMERICA

Tijuana
Ciudad Juárez
Sonoran Desert
Guadalupe I.
Chihuahua
Cedros I.
Lower California
Gulf of California
Conchos R.
Sierra Madre
Mexican Plateau
Falcon L.
Torreón
Monterrey
Rio Grande
M E X I C O
Marías Islands
Panuco R.
León
Guadalajara
L. Chapala
Mexico City
Puebl
Popocatépetl ▲ 17,888 ft
Citlo 18,7
Balsas R.
Acapulco
P A C I F I C   O C E A

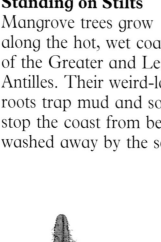

Standing on Stilts
Mangrove trees grow along the hot, wet coasts of the Greater and Lesser Antilles. Their weird-looking roots trap mud and so help stop the coast from being washed away by the sea.

Nearly every place along the west side of Central America has been affected by an earthquake or volcano at some time.

Hot Spots
Hot deserts, such as the Sonoran, cover much of northern Mexico. These dry lands are dotted with cacti – prickly plants that survive by storing water in their swollen stems.

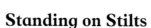

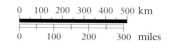

0   100 200 300 400 500 km

0   100   200   300 miles

N
W   E
S

Valuable Discoveries
Many tasty foods were first grown in this region.

Red pepper (Capsicum)

Avocado

Red sweet potato

Maize

Blowing in the Wind
Beaches in the Dominican Republic, like most Caribbean coasts, are fringed with palms. These trees bend easily, so they survive very strong winds, such as hurricanes, that blast over these islands.

The Great Bahama Bank is a huge, sandy ridge under the sea.

Pitch In
Things that fall into this lake on the island of Trinidad meet a sticky end! Thick, black asphalt, the substance that is used to build roads, slowly flows in to the lake from under the ground.

Thick tropical rain forests stretch from the Yucatán Peninsula through the southern half of Central America and into South America.

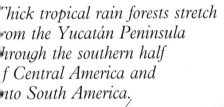

The Panama Canal is just 40 miles (64 km) long. It cuts across the narrowest part of Central America.

Grand Bahama I.
Great Abaco I.
Nassau
Andros I.
BAHAMAS
Straits of Florida
Great Bahama Bank
Tropic of Cancer
ATLANTIC OCEAN
Havana
CUBA
Turks & Caicos Islands (to U.K.)
Isle of Pines
Holguín
Santiago de Cuba
Windward Passage
HAITI
DOMINICAN REPUBLIC
Port-au-Prince
San Juan
Virgin Islands (to U.K./U.S.A.)
Santo Domingo
Anguilla (to U.K)
Puerto Rico (to U.S.A.)
ST. KITTS & NEVIS
ANTIGUA & BARBUDA
Montserrat (to U.K.)
Guadeloupe (to France)
DOMINICA
Martinique (to France)
ST. LUCIA
ST. VINCENT & THE GRENADINES
Bridgetown
BARBADOS
GRENADA
Netherlands Antilles (to Netherlands)
TRINIDAD & TOBAGO
Port of Spain
Greater Antilles
Lesser Antilles
Caribbean Sea
Aruba (to Netherlands)
Kingston
JAMAICA
Cayman Islands (to U.K.)
Cozumel I.
Yucatán Channel
Mérida
Yucatán Peninsula
Gulf of Mexico
BELIZE
Belmopan
Gulf of Honduras
GUATEMALA
Guatemala City
HONDURAS
Tegucigalpa
Coco R.
San Salvador
EL SALVADOR
NICARAGUA
León
Managua
L. Nicaragua
COSTA RICA
San José
Panama Canal
Panama City
Gulf of Darien
Coronado Bay
PANAMA
Gulf of Panama
Gulf of Chiriquí
COLOMBIA
VENEZUELA

SOUTH AMERICA

The spectacular continent of South America contains some of Earth's most amazing places. In the north, the mighty Amazon River powers through the hot, wet rain forest on its journey to the Atlantic Ocean. Traveling south, tropical forests give way to the grassy lands of the Pampas and then to the cold, high Patagonian plateau. A long chain of mountains, called the Andes, towers above the Pacific coast.

Animals of the Amazon

Morpho butterfly

Toco toucan

Woolly spider monkey

Giant armadillo

Secrets in the Jungle

Amazonia covers more than 2.4 million square miles (6 million km²). It is the world's largest tropical rain forest. This gigantic jungle is home to more species than anywhere else on Earth.

Meeting of the Waters

The muddy, brown Amazon River joins the clear, dark Negro River near Manaus in Brazil. Like oil and water, these different waters do not mix well – a line of swirls marks the place where they meet.

Far to Fall

Angel Falls in Venezuela is the tallest waterfall on Earth. Water drops off a cliff and falls 3,212 feet (979 m). This is 18 times higher than Niagara Falls in North America!

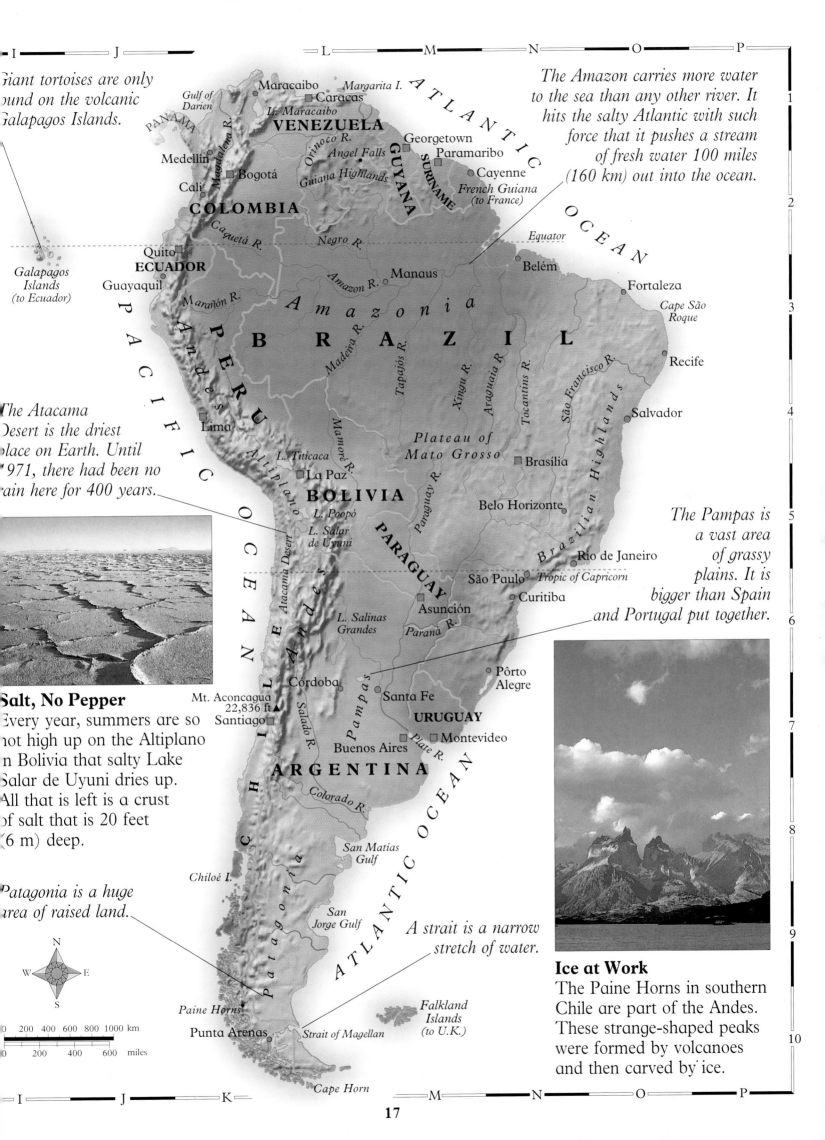

Giant tortoises are only found on the volcanic Galapagos Islands.

The Amazon carries more water to the sea than any other river. It hits the salty Atlantic with such force that it pushes a stream of fresh water 100 miles (160 km) out into the ocean.

Galapagos Islands (to Ecuador)

The Atacama Desert is the driest place on Earth. Until 1971, there had been no rain here for 400 years.

Salt, No Pepper
Every year, summers are so hot high up on the Altiplano in Bolivia that salty Lake Salar de Uyuni dries up. All that is left is a crust of salt that is 20 feet (6 m) deep.

Patagonia is a huge area of raised land.

The Pampas is a vast area of grassy plains. It is bigger than Spain and Portugal put together.

A strait is a narrow stretch of water.

Ice at Work
The Paine Horns in southern Chile are part of the Andes. These strange-shaped peaks were formed by volcanoes and then carved by ice.

Map labels

ATLANTIC OCEAN
PACIFIC OCEAN
PANAMA
Gulf of Darien
Maracaibo
L. Maracaibo
Caracas
Margarita I.
VENEZUELA
Medellín
Magdalena R.
Bogotá
Cali
COLOMBIA
Orinoco R.
Angel Falls
Guiana Highlands
GUYANA
SURINAME
Georgetown
Paramaribo
Cayenne
French Guiana (to France)
Caquetá R.
Negro R.
Equator
Quito
ECUADOR
Guayaquil
Marañón R.
Amazon R.
Manaus
Belém
Fortaleza
Cape São Roque
A m a z o n i a
PERU
B R A Z I L
Madeira R.
Tapajós R.
Xingu R.
Araguaia R.
Tocantins R.
São Francisco R.
Recife
Andes
Lima
L. Titicaca
Mamoré R.
Plateau of Mato Grosso
Brazilian Highlands
Salvador
La Paz
Altiplano
BOLIVIA
L. Poopó
L. Salar de Uyuni
Paraguay R.
Brasília
Belo Horizonte
Atacama Desert
PARAGUAY
Rio de Janeiro
São Paulo
Tropic of Capricorn
Curitiba
Andes
L. Salinas Grandes
Paraná
Pôrto Alegre
Córdoba
Santa Fe
URUGUAY
Mt. Aconcagua 22,836 ft
Santiago
Pampas
Salado R.
Montevideo
Buenos Aires
Plate R.
CHILE
ARGENTINA
Colorado R.
San Matías Gulf
Chiloé I.
Patagonia
San Jorge Gulf
Falkland Islands (to U.K.)
Paine Horns
Punta Arenas
Strait of Magellan
Cape Horn

Compass & scale

N
W   E
S

0 200 400 600 800 1000 km
0 200 400 600 miles

NORTHERN AFRICA

Almost all of northern Africa lies north of the equator. The center of this half of the African continent is filled by the Earth's largest and hottest desert – the Sahara. This sandy region stretches from the Atlantic Ocean to the Red Sea. The northwest edge of this huge, dry area rises up into the high, snowy Atlas Mountains. As you move toward the equator, the weather is wetter, and hot desert changes into grassland and then to thick tropical rain forest.

Any place in the desert where water reaches the surface, such as Tamanrasset in Algeria, is known as an oasis.

CAPE VERDE

Tree-mendous Tropics
The trees in Cameroon stand 100 feet (30 m) tall, their tops almost touching. Little sunlight gets through this leafy roof to reach the forest floor.

The Sahel is a strip of tropical grassland that lies between the dry Sahara and the wet rain forests to the south.

M e d i t e r r

Ceuta
(to Spain)
Melilla
(to Spain)
Algiers
Tunis
Tangier
Constantine
Oran
TUNISIA
Casablanca
Rabat
Sfax
Marrakesh
T
Al' Azīzīyah
Atlas Mountains

MOROCCO

A L G E R I A

El Aaiún

*S a h a r a
D e s e r t*

WESTERN SAHARA

Fdérik
Tamanrasset Oasis
*Ahaggar
Mountains*

L
Wa

A T L A N T I C   O C E A N

MAURITANIA
Nouakchott

M A L I
Timbuktu

N I G E R
Agadez

S   a   h   e   l

Senegal R.

SENEGAL
Dakar
GAMBIA
Banjul
Praia

Niger R.

Niamey

Bamako
Ouagadougou
N'Djame
Bissau
**GUINEA-
BISSAU**
GUINEA
BURKINA
NIGERIA
Conakry
Freetown
SIERRA LEONE
**CÔTE
D'IVOIRE**
Monrovia
LIBERIA
Yamoussoukro
GHANA
TOGO
BENIN
Porto-Novo
Niger R.
Abuja
Lomé
Lagos
Abidjan
Accra
A d a m a w
Highlan
CAMEROO
Yaoundé

Gulf of Guinea

**EQUATORIAL
GUINEA**

N
W   E
S

GABON

0   200   400   600   800 km

0   100   200   300   400   500 miles

18

Sand Castles in the Air

The Sahara Desert spreads over about 3.6 million square miles (9 million km²). Nearly one-quarter is covered in sand. The rest is rocky. In Libya, the hot sand is blown into dunes that can be taller than a 65-story building!

The highest temperature recorded on Earth was at Al' Azīzīyáh in Libya. It rose to 136.4°F (58°C).

Sahara's Survivors

Desert scorpion

Desert locust

Dung beetle

Common chameleon

No Soft Center

The volcanic Ahaggar Mountains in southern Algeria form a massive "island" that rises high above the surrounding sand and rock.

The Nile is the Earth's longest river. It flows for 4,140 miles (6,670 km) and brings water to dry, desert lands.

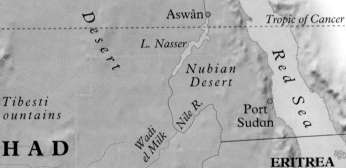

The Sudd is a huge swamp. It covers 50,000 square miles (129,500 km²) – an area about the size of England.

Weird Water

You can't drink the water that bubbles out of the ground in the Danakil Depression in Ethiopia. It is full of a smelly, yellow substance, called sulfur.

Map labels:

Benghazi · Nile Delta · Port Said · Alexandria · Cairo · Qattâra Depression · Giza · LIBYAN DESERT · LYA · EGYPT · Aswân · Tropic of Cancer · L. Nasser · Nubian Desert · Nile R. · Red Sea · Tibesti Mountains · Port Sudan · Wadi el Milk · CHAD · ERITREA · Omdurman · Khartoum · Asmara · Blue Nile · Danakil Depression · White Nile · L. Tana · DJIBOUTI · Djibouti · Gulf of Aden · SUDAN · Ethiopian Highlands · Addis Ababa · Hargeysa · Sarh · Sudd · ETHIOPIA · Shebeli R. · SOMALIA · CENTRAL AFRICAN REPUBLIC · L. Turkana · Juba R. · Bangui · ZAIRE · UGANDA · KENYA · Mogadishu · INDIAN OCEAN · Equator · Mediterranean Sea

19

SOUTHERN AFRICA

The southern half of Africa is a jigsaw of different climates. Near the equator in the Congo Basin, it is hot and wet. This weather is ideal for tropical rain forests. As you travel south, the climate gets drier, and thick jungles give way to savanna – vast, open grasslands with scattered trees. Toward the southwest of southern Africa, it is so dry that there are large, sandy deserts.

Thundering Down
The slow, sleepy Zambezi River tips over a high, wide ledge of rock at Victoria Falls. Local people call this waterfall "The Smoke That Thunders" because it makes so much spray and noise.

Super Swamp
The Okavango River never reaches the sea. Instead, its waters empty into a vast area of flat land in Botswana to form a swampy delta.

Sea fog travels up to 12 miles (20 km) inland each night and waters the few plants that manage to survive in the hot, sandy Namib Desert.

Table for a Giant
Table Mountain, which towers above Cape Town, has a flat top. When clouds roll over it, the "table" looks as if it is covered by a tablecloth!

The climate and plants at the tip of Africa are similar to those found around the Mediterranean Sea.

Malabo
Bioko
CAMEROON
SAO TOME & PRINCIPE
EQUATORIAL GUINEA
São Tomé
Libreville
Port-Gentil
GABON
CENTRAL AFRIC... REPUBLIC
Ubangi R.
CONGO
Congo R.
Oubangui R.
Con...
Bas...
ZAIR...
Brazzaville
Pointe-Noire
Kinshasa
Cabinda
Kananga
Mbuji-M...
ATLANTIC OCEAN
Luanda
Cuanza R.
ANGOLA
Huambo
Cunene R.
Okavango R.
Cape Fria
Namib Desert
NAMIBIA
Okav... ...
Walvis Bay
Windhoek
Kalah...
Deser...
Fish R.
SO...
Orange R.
AF...
Cape Tow...
Table Mt. 3,...
Cape of Good Hope

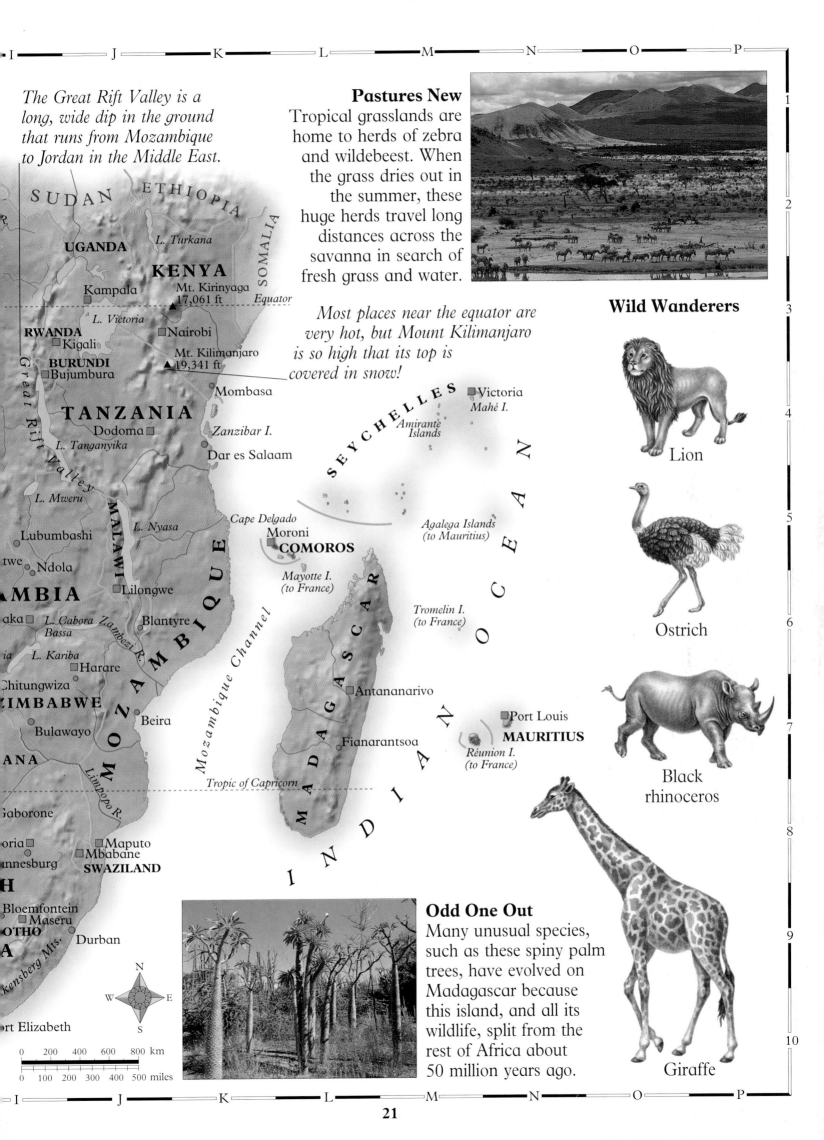

The Great Rift Valley is a long, wide dip in the ground that runs from Mozambique to Jordan in the Middle East.

Pastures New
Tropical grasslands are home to herds of zebra and wildebeest. When the grass dries out in the summer, these huge herds travel long distances across the savanna in search of fresh grass and water.

Most places near the equator are very hot, but Mount Kilimanjaro is so high that its top is covered in snow!

Wild Wanderers

Lion

Ostrich

Black rhinoceros

Giraffe

Odd One Out
Many unusual species, such as these spiny palm trees, have evolved on Madagascar because this island, and all its wildlife, split from the rest of Africa about 50 million years ago.

SUDAN

ETHIOPIA

UGANDA

L. Turkana

KENYA

SOMALIA

Kampala

Mt. Kirinyaga 17,061 ft

Equator

L. Victoria

RWANDA

Nairobi

Kigali

Mt. Kilimanjaro 19,341 ft

BURUNDI

Bujumbura

Mombasa

TANZANIA

Dodoma

Zanzibar I.

L. Tanganyika

Dar es Salaam

SEYCHELLES

Victoria

Mahé I.

Amirante Islands

L. Mweru

Lubumbashi

L. Nyasa

MALAWI

Cape Delgado

Agalega Islands (to Mauritius)

twe

Ndola

Moroni

COMOROS

AMBIA

Lilongwe

Mayotte I. (to France)

MADAGASCAR

INDIAN OCEAN

aka

L. Cabora Bassa

Zambezi R.

Blantyre

Tromelin I. (to France)

ia

L. Kariba

Harare

Antananarivo

Mozambique Channel

ZIMBABWE

Chitungwiza

Port Louis

MAURITIUS

Beira

Bulawayo

Fianarantsoa

Réunion I. (to France)

ANA

Limpopo R.

Tropic of Capricorn

Gaborone

oria

Maputo

Mbabane

nnesburg

SWAZILAND

H

Bloemfontein

Maseru

OTHO

Durban

A

kensberg Mts.

N W E S

rt Elizabeth

0 200 400 600 800 km
0 100 200 300 400 500 miles

MOZAMBIQUE

Great Rift Valley

21

NORTHERN EUROPE

Norway and Sweden sit on a piece of land separated from most of Finland by the Gulf of Bothnia. These are countries with huge forests and spectacular lakes, with snow covering the mountains toward the north. The climate gets milder in Denmark and southern Sweden. The west coast of Norway is also mild because it is warmed by a current of water called the North Atlantic Drift, which travels across the ocean from North America.

Hot Below, Cold Above

Iceland is not as cold as it looks. Heat from the Earth's center escapes, melting the edges of Iceland's great ice sheet, called Vatnajökull, to make chilly lakes.

Lights in the Sky

The skies in the extreme north are sometimes lit up by colorful, shimmering lights. This is called an aurora. It is caused by a stream of electrically charged particles that come from the sun.

Way, way out in the cold North Atlantic Ocean, there are 18 volcanic islands called the Faeroes. Even farther still is the large island of Iceland.

A Scotch pine tree grows by Lake Inari.

Green Giants

| Aspen (65 ft / 20 m) | Silver birch (98 ft / 30 m) | Scotch pine (114 ft / 35 m) | Norway spruce (164 ft / 50 m) |

Lapping Waters

Lake Inari is a vast lake that lies in the north of Finland. It is so big that more than 3,000 tiny forested islands sit in its waters. In places it is deep enough to cover a 22-story building.

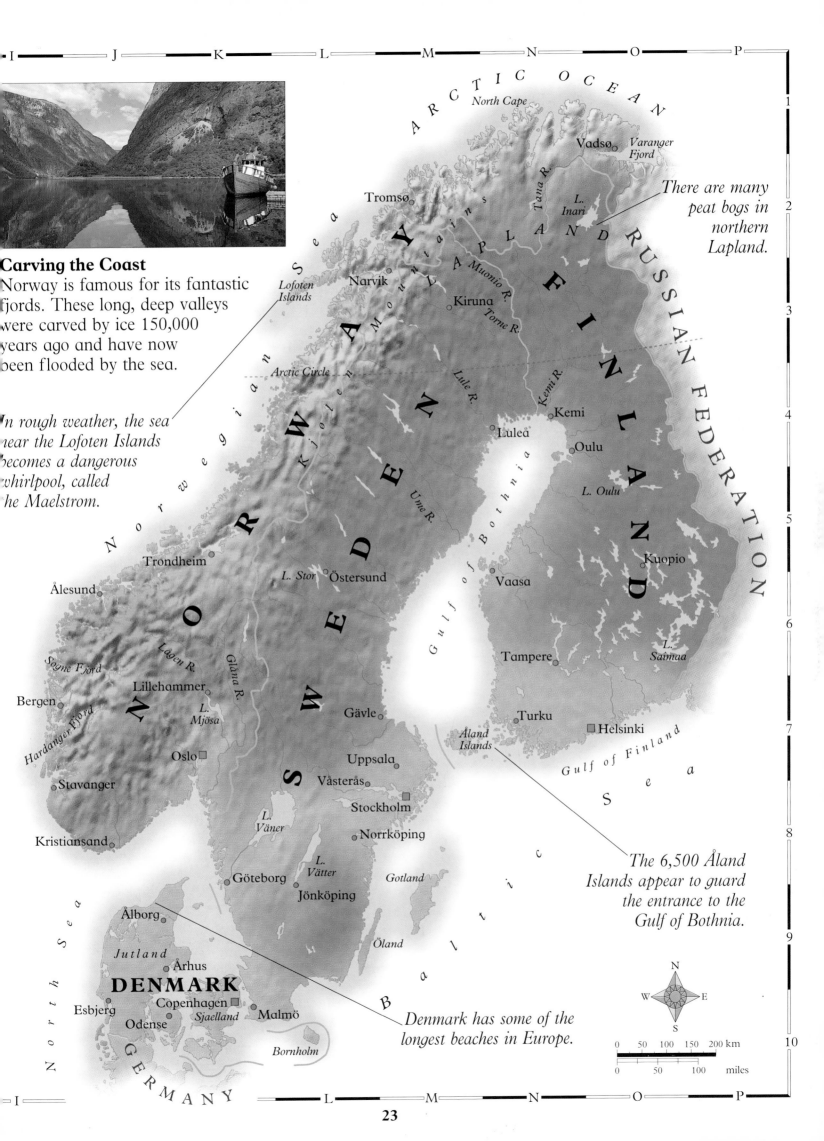

Carving the Coast

Norway is famous for its fantastic fjords. These long, deep valleys were carved by ice 150,000 years ago and have now been flooded by the sea.

In rough weather, the sea near the Lofoten Islands becomes a dangerous whirlpool, called the Maelstrom.

There are many peat bogs in northern Lapland.

ARCTIC OCEAN

North Cape

Vadsø

Varanger Fjord

Tromsø

Tana R.

L. Inari

RUSSIAN FEDERATION

Narvik

Lofoten Islands

Kjølen Mountains

Lapland

Muonio R.

Kiruna

Torne R.

Arctic Circle

FINLAND

Lule R.

Kemi R.

Kemi

Luleå

Oulu

Gulf of Bothnia

L. Oulu

NORWAY

SWEDEN

Ume R.

Kuopio

Trondheim

L. Stor

Östersund

Vaasa

L. Saimaa

Ålesund

Tampere

Sogne Fjord

Lågen R.

Glåma R.

Turku

Helsinki

Bergen

Lillehammer

L. Mjösa

Gävle

Åland Islands

Gulf of Finland

Hardanger Fjord

Stavanger

Oslo

Uppsala

Våsterås

Stockholm

Baltic Sea

The 6,500 Åland Islands appear to guard the entrance to the Gulf of Bothnia.

Kristiansand

L. Väner

Norrköping

L. Vätter

Gotland

Göteborg

Jönköping

Öland

Ålborg

Jutland

Århus

DENMARK

Copenhagen

Esbjerg

Sjaelland

Malmö

Odense

Bornholm

GERMANY

North Sea

Norwegian Sea

Denmark has some of the longest beaches in Europe.

N
W E
S

0 50 100 150 200 km

0   50   100   miles

WESTERN EUROPE

The part of Europe that lies farthest away from Asia is known as western Europe. The coasts that face the cool Atlantic Ocean are wet and windy. Inland, away from the sea, it is usually drier and less stormy. Generally, the farther south you travel in western Europe, the hotter it becomes. By the time you reach the shores of the Mediterranean Sea, the summers are hot and dry.

Into the Woods
The climate in the United Kingdom is temperate. This means that it is never too hot or too cold, and there is plenty of rain for beech and oak trees.

Classic Columns
More than 60 million years ago, boiling hot lava slowly poured out of the ocean floor near Northern Ireland. The lava cooled into tall columns of rock, called the Giant's Causeway.

Woodland Wanderers

Pipistrelle bat

European stoat

European badger

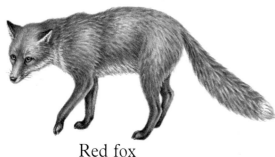

Red fox

Strong Skittles
Although they are called the Ninepins, you could never bowl over these rugged rocks! They lie in northeast Spain among the Sierra de Loarre.

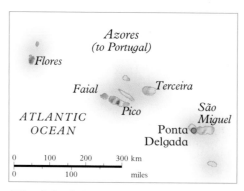

Azores
(to Portugal)

Flores

Faial　　　Terceira

Pico　　　São Miguel

ATLANTIC OCEAN

Ponta Delgada

0　100　200　300 km

0　100　miles

The Madeira Islands lie 560 miles (900 km) off Portugal. The Azores are more remote, they lie one-third of the way to North America.

Madeira Islands
(to Portugal)　　Porto Santo

Madeira

ATLANTIC OCEAN

0　100　200 km

0　100　miles

The Canary Islands lie 870 miles (1,400 km) off the southwest coast of Spain.

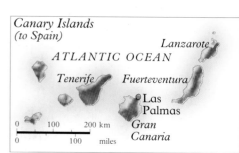

Canary Islands
(to Spain)

Lanzarote

ATLANTIC OCEAN

Tenerife　　Fuerteventura

Las Palmas

Gran Canaria

0　100　200 km

0　100　miles

The west coast of Scotland is warmed by a current of water, called the North Atlantic Drift.

Shetland Islands

Orkney Islands

Outer Hebrides

Grampian Mts. •Aberdeen

Inner Hebrides SCOTLAND

Glasgow •Edinburgh

Giant's Causeway •Newcastle upon Tyne

NORTHERN IRELAND UNITED KINGDOM

Belfast Leeds

REPUBLIC OF IRELAND Irish Sea Liverpool Manchester Sheffield

Shannon R. Dublin

Cork

Ireland has lots of peat bogs.

WALES R. Severn •Birmingham ENGLAND

Cardiff R. Thames □London

Bristol

English Channel

Channel Islands

ATLANTIC

OCEAN

Mont St. Michel

F R A N C E

Loire R. •Orléans

Nantes

Portugal and Spain sit on a square-shaped piece of land, called the Iberian Peninsula.

Bay of Biscay

Dordogne R. Massif Central

Bordeaux

Garonne R. Grotte de Clamouse

Toulouse

Bilbao Pyrenees ANDORRA

Cantábrica Mountains Ebro R. Sierra de Loarre

Valladolid Zaragoza

Porto Barcelona

S P A I N

Douro R.

PORTUGAL Madrid□ Tagus R.

Iberian Peninsula Majorca

Guadiana R. •Valencia

□Lisbon Balearic Islands

Sierra Morena Guadalquivir R.

Lagos

•Sevilla Sierra Nevada

Málaga Mediterranean Sea

Gulf of Cádiz Gibraltar (to U.K.)

Strait of Gibraltar

North Sea NETHERLANDS

The Hague □Amsterdam Utrecht

Rotterdam

Part of the Netherlands is on a large river delta, which the sea is always trying to wash away.

•Antwerp GERMANY

Brussels□

Lille BELGIUM

Seine R. LUXEMBOURG

Marne R. Meuse R.

□Paris •Strasbourg

Saône R. SWITZERLAND

L. Geneva Mont Blanc ▲15,772 ft

Lyon ALPS

Rhône R. ITALY

Nice• MONACO

•Marseille

Corsica (to France) •Ajaccio

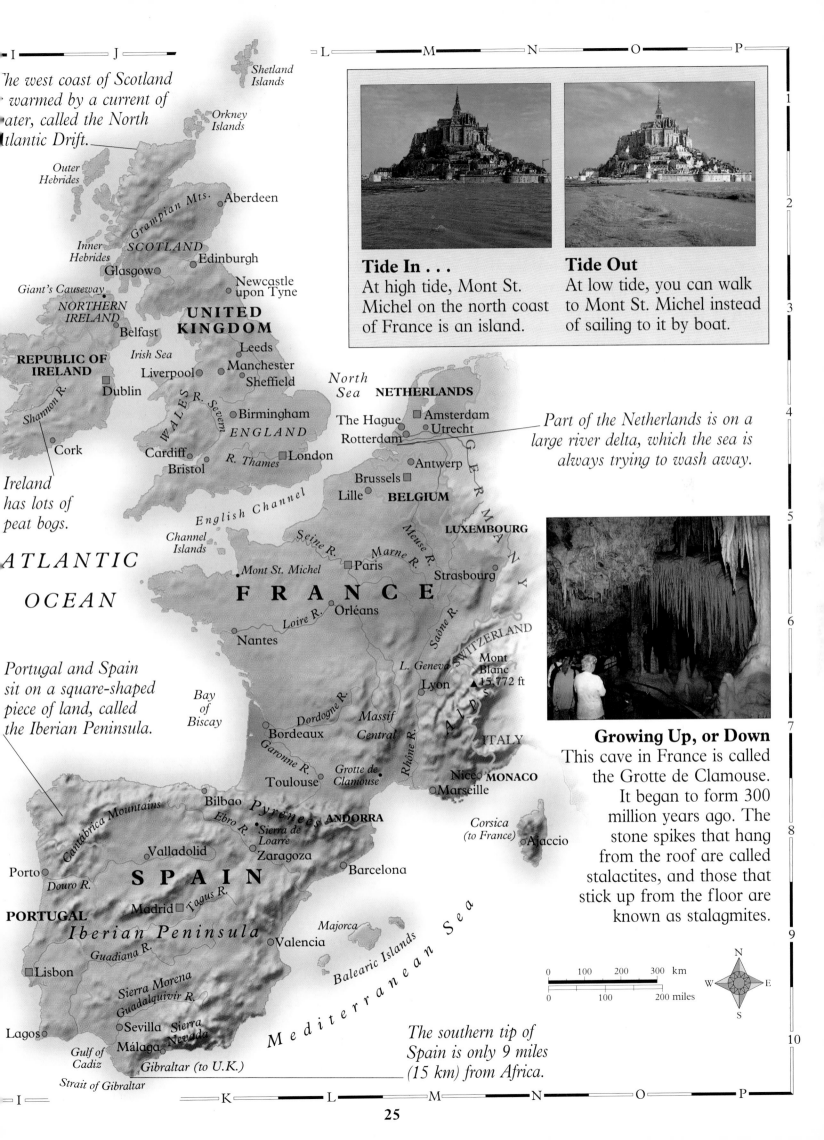

Tide In . . .
At high tide, Mont St. Michel on the north coast of France is an island.

Tide Out
At low tide, you can walk to Mont St. Michel instead of sailing to it by boat.

Growing Up, or Down
This cave in France is called the Grotte de Clamouse. It began to form 300 million years ago. The stone spikes that hang from the roof are called stalactites, and those that stick up from the floor are known as stalagmites.

0 100 200 300 km
0 100 200 miles

N
W E
S

The southern tip of Spain is only 9 miles (15 km) from Africa.

25

1
3
4
5
6
7
8
9
10

CENTRAL EUROPE

The land that stretches from the Baltic Sea to the Mediterranean Sea is known as central Europe. Halfway down, it is cut in two by a range of snow-covered mountains, called the Alps. The area to the north of this divide includes the cool, forested plains of Germany and Poland. Italy, to the south, is a long peninsula of land surrounded by warm seas such as the Mediterranean.

Road of Water
Ships can sail all the way up the Rhine River, through Germany, to Switzerland. The river runs through many green valleys on its long journey of 820 miles (1,320 km).

Alpine Plants

Alpine aster   King of the Alps

The Hills Are Alive
During the spring, these slopes are a mass of colorful alpine flowers. They have survived the cold winter frosts by being covered by a thick blanket of snow.

Slipping Away
Some of the snow on top of the Swiss Alps freezes into rivers of ice, called glaciers. Each glacier slowly slips down the mountain. When they reach the warm lower slopes, they melt into streams.

Mediterranean Plants

Wild sage   Poppy

Summer Survivors
The poppies growing on this coast in southern Italy can live without much water. Plants that grow around the Mediterranean Sea have to survive hot, dry summers.

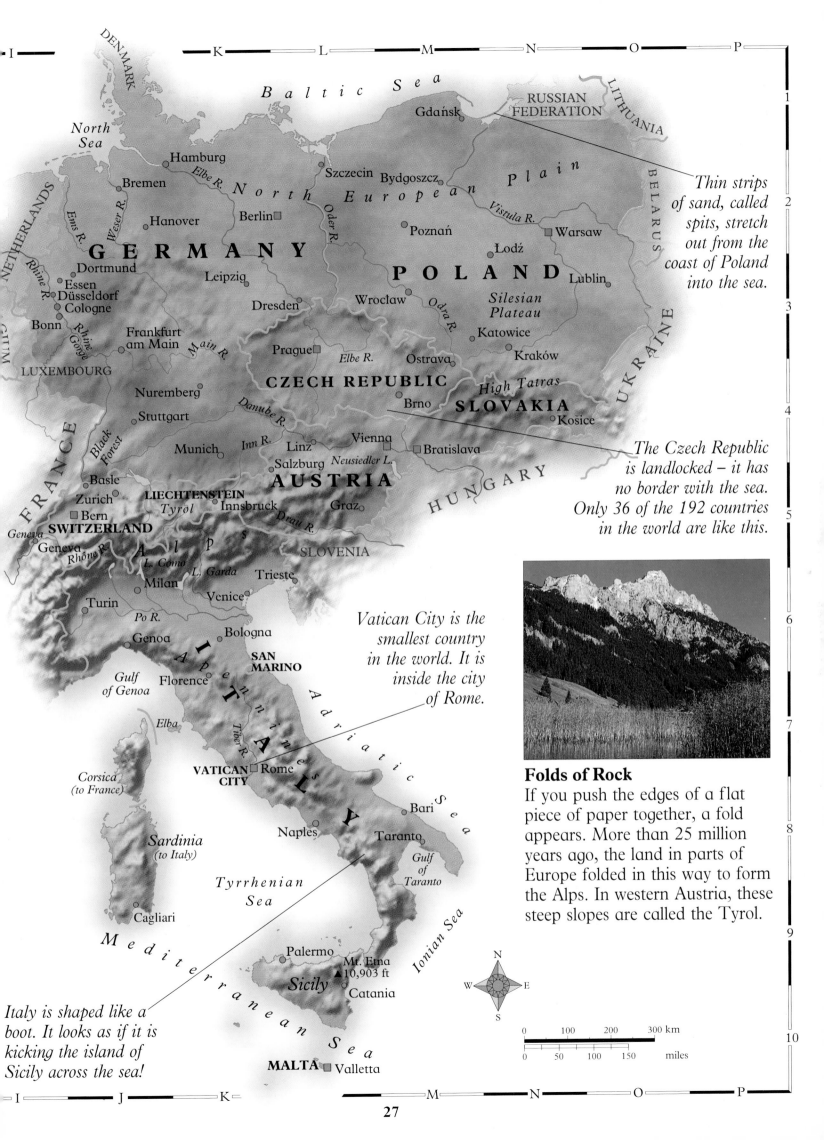

Thin strips of sand, called spits, stretch out from the coast of Poland into the sea.

The Czech Republic is landlocked – it has no border with the sea. Only 36 of the 192 countries in the world are like this.

Vatican City is the smallest country in the world. It is inside the city of Rome.

Folds of Rock

If you push the edges of a flat piece of paper together, a fold appears. More than 25 million years ago, the land in parts of Europe folded in this way to form the Alps. In western Austria, these steep slopes are called the Tyrol.

Italy is shaped like a boot. It looks as if it is kicking the island of Sicily across the sea!

EASTERN EUROPE

The eastern side of Europe is dotted with many large lakes and small seas. It is a land of contrasts. The northern half is cold and fairly flat and mostly taken up by one enormous country, the Russian Federation. The southern half of eastern Europe is quite different. It is warmer, more mountainous, and split into many smaller countries, such as Moldova and Macedonia. This southern region is also much more likely to be shaken by earthquakes.

Nice Spots

The Adriatic Sea is very slowly flooding the southwest corner of eastern Europe. Gradually, low land disappears under the waves, leaving only the tops of hills above water level. This type of coast is called a dalmatian coast.

When it freezes in winter, you can walk on the White Sea.

Many rare wetland birds nest among the reeds and rushes of the Pripet Marshes.

Worn Out

Water can carve through rock! A river on Crete has cut out the Samaria Gorge. This deep valley twists and turns its way through the land for 11 miles (18 km).

Greece has so many inlets along its coastline that no place is more than 60 miles (100 km) away from the sea.

N W E S

| 0 | 200 | 400 | 600 km |
| 0 | 100 | 200 | 300 | miles |

NORWAY
FINLAND
L. Bele
L. Or.
L. Ladoga
Gulf of Finland
Baltic Sea
Tallinn St. Peters
ESTONIA
LATVIA
Riga Western Dvina R.
North
LITHUANIA
Kaliningrad
RUSS. FED. Vilnius
Minsk
BELARUS
POLAND
Pripet R. Pripet Marshes
Chernobyl
Kiev
UKRAIN
SLOVAKIA Carpathian Mts.
AUSTRIA
MOLDOVA
Budapest Chisnāu
SLOVENIA HUNGARY ROMANIA
Ljubljana
Zagreb Transylvanian Alps Odesa
CROATIA YUGOSLAVIA
BOSNIA-HERZEGOVINA Belgrade Bucharest
Sarajevo Danube R.
Adriatic Sea BULGARIA Black
Tirana Sofia
Skopje
MACEDONIA
ALBANIA Thessaloniki
Aegean Sea TURKE
Athens
Samaria Gorge Crete
GREECE
Mediterranean Sea
ITALY

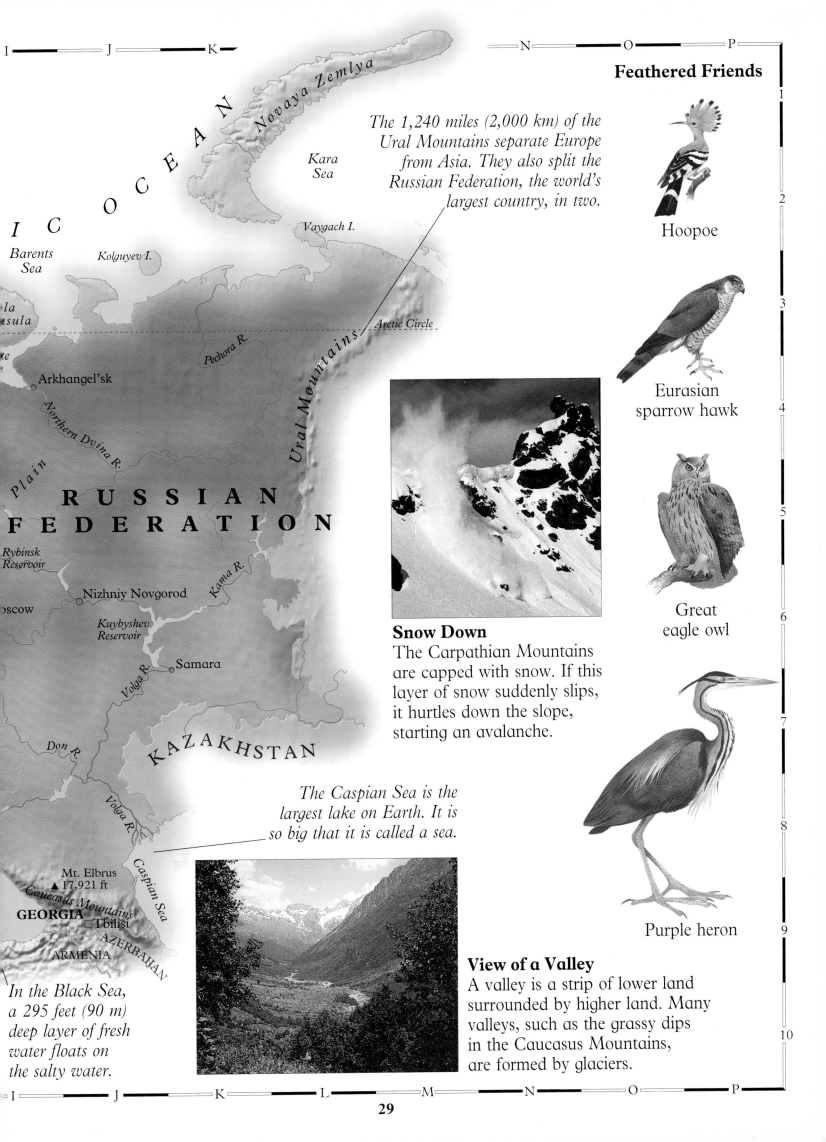

I   J   K   N   O   P

A R C T I C   O C E A N

Novaya Zemlya

Kara Sea

Vaygach I.

Barents Sea

Kolguyev I.

...la ...sula

The 1,240 miles (2,000 km) of the Ural Mountains separate Europe from Asia. They also split the Russian Federation, the world's largest country, in two.

Hoopoe

Arctic Circle

Pechora R.

Ural Mountains

Eurasian sparrow hawk

Arkhangel'sk

Northern Dvina R.

Plain

R U S S I A N
F E D E R A T I O N

Great eagle owl

Rybinsk Reservoir

...scow

Nizhniy Novgorod

Kama R.

Kuybyshev Reservoir

Snow Down
The Carpathian Mountains are capped with snow. If this layer of snow suddenly slips, it hurtles down the slope, starting an avalanche.

Volga R.

Samara

K A Z A K H S T A N

Don R.

The Caspian Sea is the largest lake on Earth. It is so big that it is called a sea.

Volga R.

Purple heron

Mt. Elbrus
▲ *17,921 ft*

Caucasus Mountains

Caspian Sea

GEORGIA □*Tbilisi*

AZERBAIJAN

ARMENIA

In the Black Sea, a 295 feet (90 m) deep layer of fresh water floats on the salty water.

View of a Valley
A valley is a strip of lower land surrounded by higher land. Many valleys, such as the grassy dips in the Caucasus Mountains, are formed by glaciers.

I   J   K   L   M   N   O   P

THE MIDDLE EAST

The lands that lie where Africa, Europe, and Asia meet are known as the Middle East. Almost all the southern half of this region is covered by sand and rocks. Here there are vast, hot, dry deserts – places where few plants survive. Many of the mountains and plateaus to the north are just as dry. It is only when you travel toward the shores of the Mediterranean Sea that there is more rain.

BULGARIA
GREECE
Aegean Sea
Istanbul
Sea of Marmara
Bursa
Izmir
Pamu
Mediterrane

White Wonderland
At Pamukkale, in Turkey, a warm stream of water and minerals bubbles out of the ground. The minerals left behind by the water have formed a stairway of white, stone steps.

Salty Sea
The Dead Sea, which lies between Israel and Jordan, is the lowest place on Earth. It is about 1,310 feet (400 m) lower than the surface of the nearby Mediterranean Sea. It is also the saltiest area of water on Earth. The water is so salty that no fish can survive in it.

Stones cover the desert floor.

Stony Heart
Much of central Iran is a cold, hilly desert. Strong winds have blown away most of the sand to leave a bare, stony pavement.

Desert Dwellers

Arabian oryx   Egyptian vulture   Camel

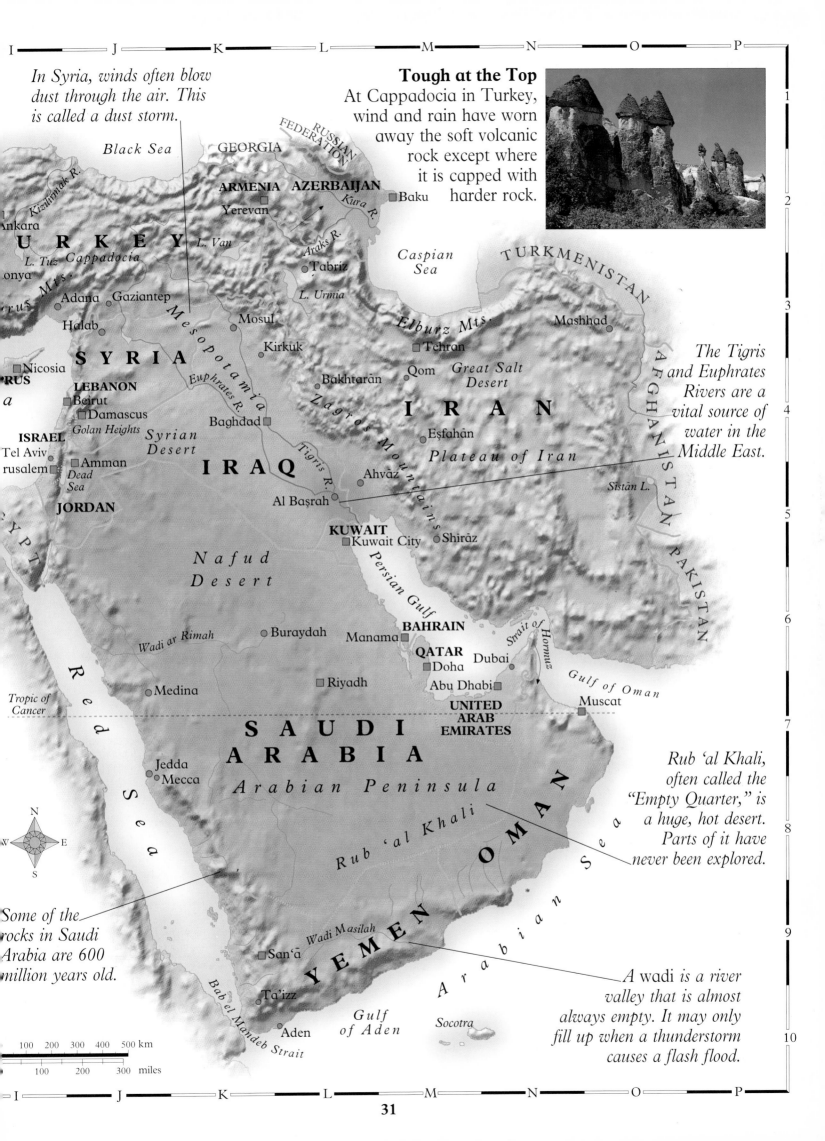

In Syria, winds often blow dust through the air. This is called a dust storm.

Tough at the Top
At Cappadocia in Turkey, wind and rain have worn away the soft volcanic rock except where it is capped with harder rock.

The Tigris and Euphrates Rivers are a vital source of water in the Middle East.

Rub 'al Khali, often called the "Empty Quarter," is a huge, hot desert. Parts of it have never been explored.

Some of the rocks in Saudi Arabia are 600 million years old.

A wadi is a river valley that is almost always empty. It may only fill up when a thunderstorm causes a flash flood.

Grid columns: I J K L M N O P (top and bottom)
Grid rows: 1 2 3 4 5 6 7 8 9 10 (right side)

Black Sea
GEORGIA
RUSSIAN FEDERATION
ARMENIA AZERBAIJAN
□ Baku
Yerevan
Kizilirmak R.
Ankara
TURKEY
L. Van
Kura R.
Araks R.
Tabriz
Cappadocia
L. Tuz
Konya
Taurus Mts.
Adana Gaziantep
Halab
Mosul
L. Urmia
Caspian Sea
TURKMENISTAN
Elburz Mts.
Mashhad
Nicosia
CYPRUS
SYRIA
Kirkuk
Tehran
Qom Great Salt Desert
IRAN
LEBANON
Beirut
Mesopotamia
Euphrates R.
Baghdad
Bakhtarān
AFGHANISTAN
Damascus
Golan Heights
Syrian Desert
Eşfahān
Plateau of Iran
ISRAEL
Tel Aviv
Jerusalem
Amman
Dead Sea
IRAQ
Zagros Mountains
Tigris R.
Ahvāz
Sistān L.
JORDAN
Al Başrah
KUWAIT
Kuwait City
Shirāz
PAKISTAN
EGYPT
Nafud Desert
Persian Gulf
Red Sea
Wadi ar Rimah
Buraydah
Manama
BAHRAIN
QATAR
Doha
Dubai
Strait of Hormuz
Gulf of Oman
Tropic of Cancer
Medina
Riyadh
Abu Dhabi
Muscat
SAUDI ARABIA
UNITED ARAB EMIRATES
Jedda
Mecca
Arabian Peninsula
OMAN
Rub 'al Khali
Arabian Sea
Wadi Masilah
San'ā
YEMEN
Ta'izz
Gulf of Aden
Socotra
Aden
Bab el Mandeb Strait

Compass: N W E S

100 200 300 400 500 km
100 200 300 miles

North & Central Asia

The world's largest forest is known as the taiga. It covers most of the cold, flat Siberian lands that stretch from the Ural Mountains to the Bering Sea. Few trees grow north of Siberia because they cannot push their roots into the frozen ground. These freezing plains of the north are called the tundra. To the south of Siberia there are cold deserts, such as the Gobi, and huge grasslands, or steppes.

Severnaya Zemlya

Kara Sea

Yamal Peninsula

Yenisey R.

Central Siberian Plateau

Ob' R.

West Siberian Plain

R U S S I A N   F E

Irtysh R.

Ob' R.

Angara R.

Yekaterinburg

Chelyabinsk

Omsk

Tomsk

Krasnoyarsk

Kustanai

Novosibirsk

Ural'sk

Aktyubinsk

Karaganda

Kirghiz Steppe

Uliastay

KAZAKHSTAN

L. Balkhash

Altai Mountains

M O

Aral Sea

Alma-Ata

Gobi D

UZBEKISTAN

Bishkek

L. Issyk-Kul'

C

Caspian Sea

Tashkent

KYRGYZSTAN

Samarkand

Osh

TURKMENISTAN

TAJIKISTAN

Ashgabat

Dushanbe

Hindu Kush

Herāt

Kabul

Khyber Pass

AFGHANISTAN

Qandahār

No Way Out
Rain rarely falls on the dry Hindu Kush mountains in Afghanistan, so this lake is a glittering prize. It is here because rocks have formed a dam across a river.

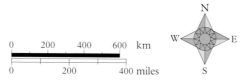

0   200   400   600   km

0   200   400 miles

N
W   E
S

Step by Step
There are many large plains in Mongolia. They are part of the enormous grasslands, called steppes, that curve across Central Asia.

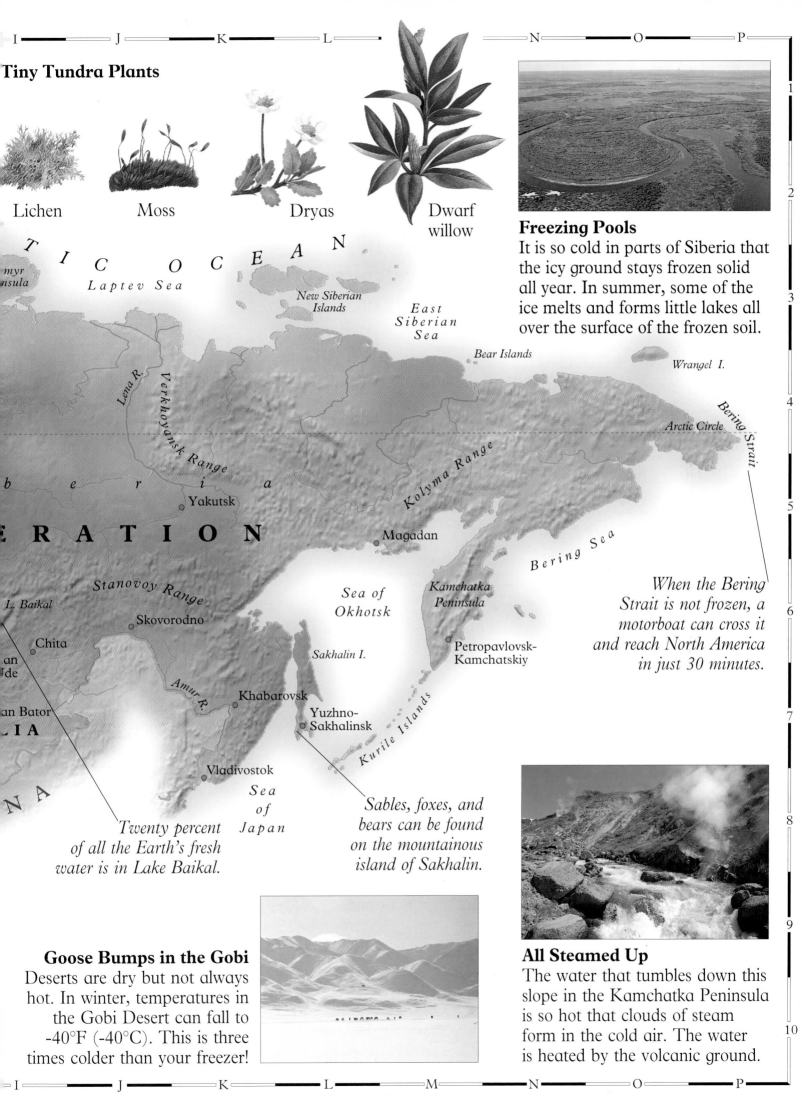

Tiny Tundra Plants

Lichen

Moss

Dryas

Dwarf willow

T I C   O C E A N

Laptev Sea

New Siberian Islands

East Siberian Sea

Bear Islands

Wrangel I.

myr nsula

Lena R.

Verkhoyansk Range

Arctic Circle

Bering Strait

Kolyma Range

Yakutsk

R A T I O N

Magadan

Bering Sea

Stanovoy Range

L. Baikal

Skovorodno

Kamchatka Peninsula

Sea of Okhotsk

Chita

Sakhalin I.

Petropavlovsk-Kamchatskiy

an Jde

an Bator

Amur R.

Khabarovsk

I A

Yuzhno-Sakhalinsk

Kurile Islands

Vladivostok

Sea of Japan

N A

Freezing Pools

It is so cold in parts of Siberia that the icy ground stays frozen solid all year. In summer, some of the ice melts and forms little lakes all over the surface of the frozen soil.

When the Bering Strait is not frozen, a motorboat can cross it and reach North America in just 30 minutes.

Sables, foxes, and bears can be found on the mountainous island of Sakhalin.

Twenty percent of all the Earth's fresh water is in Lake Baikal.

Goose Bumps in the Gobi

Deserts are dry but not always hot. In winter, temperatures in the Gobi Desert can fall to -40°F (-40°C). This is three times colder than your freezer!

All Steamed Up

The water that tumbles down this slope in the Kamchatka Peninsula is so hot that clouds of steam form in the cold air. The water is heated by the volcanic ground.

THE INDIAN SUBCONTINENT

The Himalayas are the Earth's highest mountain range. They form a vast wall of rock that splits up Asia. The triangular-shaped area to the south of this natural barrier is the Indian subcontinent. This is a region of dramatically different climates, from the cold mountains of the north to the hot deserts of the west. Each summer heavy rains fall in the eastern and southern parts, blown in by the strong monsoon winds.

Sand and rocks cover the Thar Desert. There is usually only half a yard of rain a year in this hot, dry place.

The Highest Place on Earth
Everest is the highest mountain in the world. The local people have a name for Everest that means "Mountain So High That No Bird Can Fly Over It."

Passing Over
You don't need to be a mountaineer to cross the mountains that divide Pakistan and Afghanistan. Instead, you can walk 33 miles (53 km) through the long, narrow Khyber Pass.

There are about 2,000 Maldive Islands. They are all very flat – you would be almost as tall as the highest hill!

Indian Animal Parade

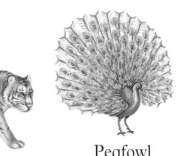

Indian elephant

King cobra

Tiger

Peafowl

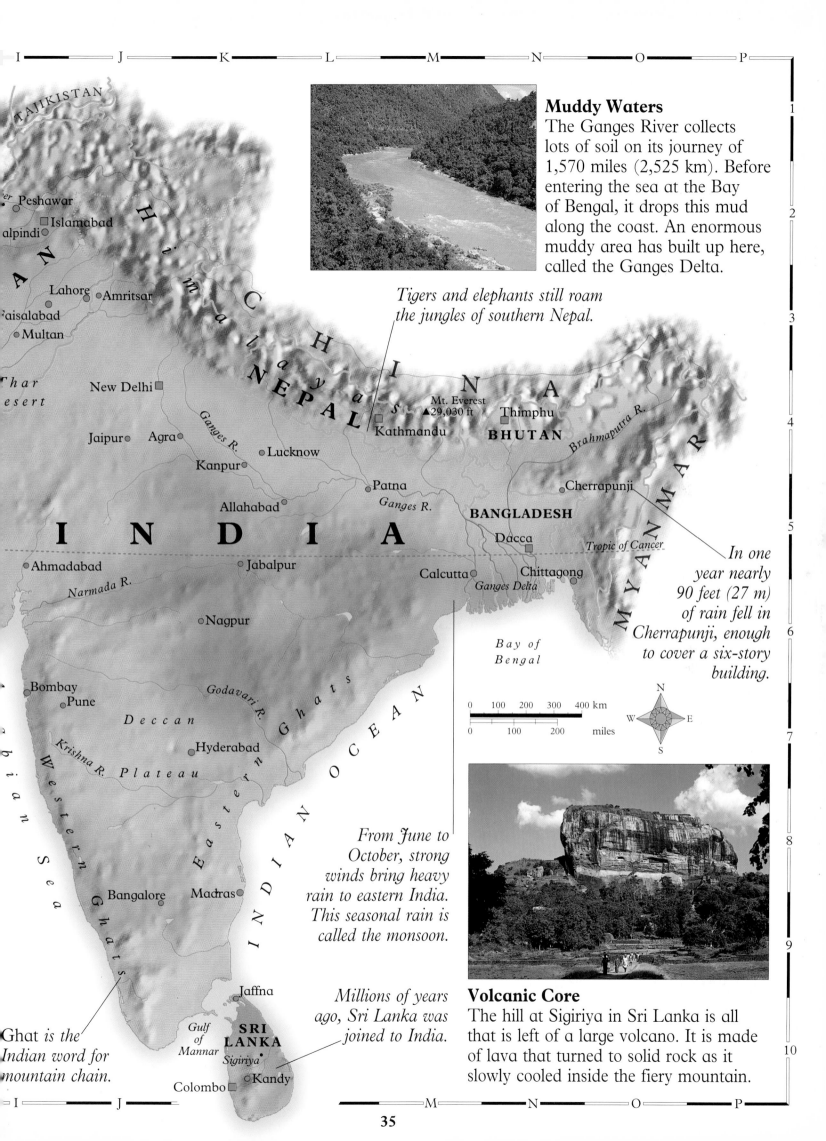

TAJIKISTAN

Peshawar

Islamabad

alpindi

Lahore ● Amritsar

aisalabad

Multan

Thar Desert

Muddy Waters

The Ganges River collects lots of soil on its journey of 1,570 miles (2,525 km). Before entering the sea at the Bay of Bengal, it drops this mud along the coast. An enormous muddy area has built up here, called the Ganges Delta.

Tigers and elephants still roam the jungles of southern Nepal.

New Delhi

NEPAL

HIMALAYA

CHINA

Mt. Everest ▲29,030 ft

Kathmandu

Thimphu

BHUTAN

Brahmaputra R.

Jaipur ● Agra

Ganges R.

Lucknow

Kanpur

Cherrapunji

Patna

Ganges R.

BANGLADESH

Allahabad

I N D I A

Dacca

Tropic of Cancer

Ahmadabad

Narmada R.

Jabalpur

Calcutta

Ganges Delta

Chittagong

MYANMAR

In one year nearly 90 feet (27 m) of rain fell in Cherrapunji, enough to cover a six-story building.

Nagpur

Bay of Bengal

Bombay ● Pune

Godavari R.

Deccan

Eastern Ghats

0　100　200　300　400 km

0　100　200　miles

N

W　　E

S

Krishna R. Plateau

Hyderabad

Western Ghats

I N D I A N   O C E A N

Bangalore

Madras

From June to October, strong winds bring heavy rain to eastern India. This seasonal rain is called the monsoon.

Arabian Sea

Jaffna

Millions of years ago, Sri Lanka was joined to India.

Volcanic Core

The hill at Sigiriya in Sri Lanka is all that is left of a large volcano. It is made of lava that turned to solid rock as it slowly cooled inside the fiery mountain.

Gulf of Mannar

SRI LANKA

Sigiriya ●

Ghat *is the Indian word for mountain chain.*

Colombo ● Kandy

EAST ASIA

China takes up most of east Asia. The cold deserts and mountains in the west of this enormous country are some of Earth's most remote places. Between this empty region and the eastern coastline there are wetter, flat, grassy plains. Farther east, the Korean Peninsula stretches out toward the islands of Japan.

The Taklamakan Desert is so hot in the summer that raindrops dry out before reaching the ground.

RUSSIAN FED.

KAZAKHSTAN

Altai Mountains

M O

Ürümqi

KYRGYZSTAN

Tienshan Mts

Tarim R.

Lop Nur L.

Taklamakan Desert

TAJIKISTAN

PAKISTAN

Kunlun Mountains

C

H

Qaidam Basin

I

Qingh

Qilian

Yellow R.

Yangtze R.

Plateau of Tibet

T I B E T

Salween R.

Mekong R.

INDIA

Brahmaputra R.

Lhasa

Himalayas

NEPAL

Mt. Everest 29,030 ft ▲

BHUTAN

INDIA

MYANMAR

Earth's Door
This "doorway" leads to an extraordinary maze of caves near Guiyang in China. These underground halls have been made by water slowly dissolving the limestone rock.

A plateau is a large area of raised land. The mountainous plateau of Tibet is the largest on Earth and is known as the "Roof of the World."

Lumpy Floor
Three hundred million years ago, fish swam over the Guilin Hills! These peaks were once the floor of an ocean. Today, they form a hilly range that is about 60 miles (100 km) long.

Exotic Plants of the East

Mulberry tree

Maidenhair tree

Wild orange tree

Bamboo grass

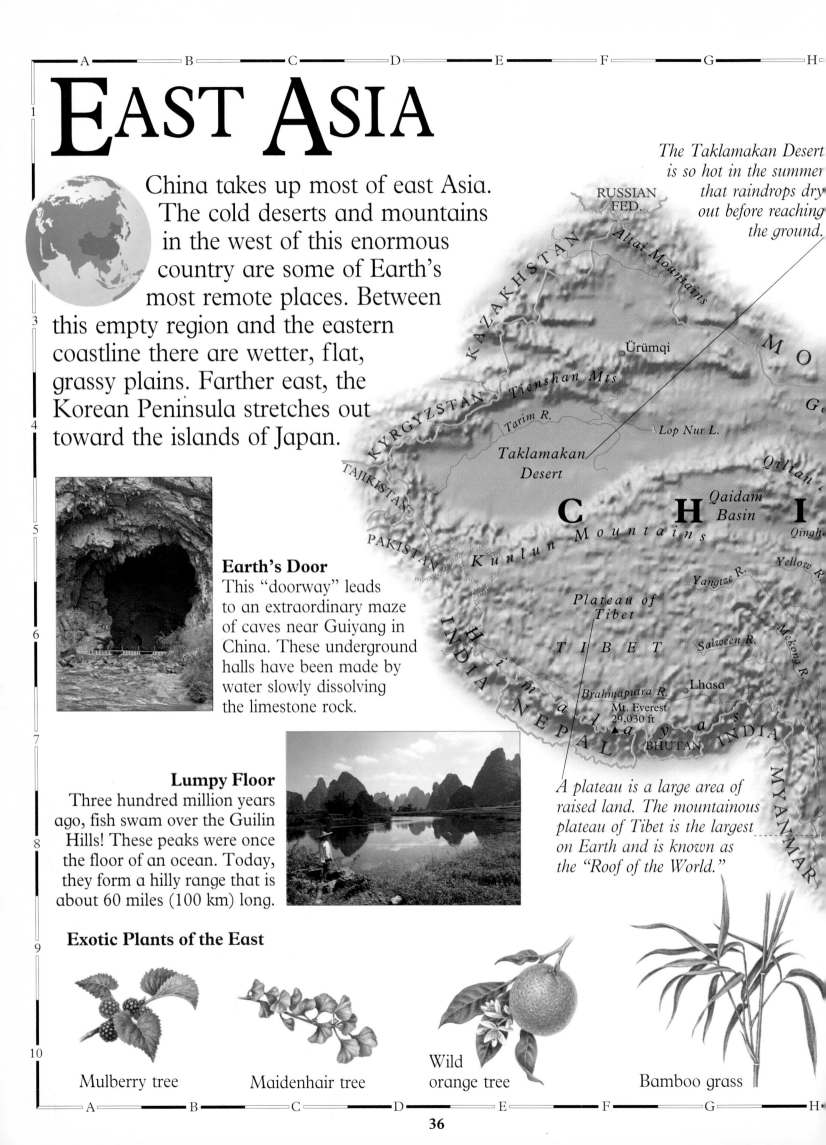

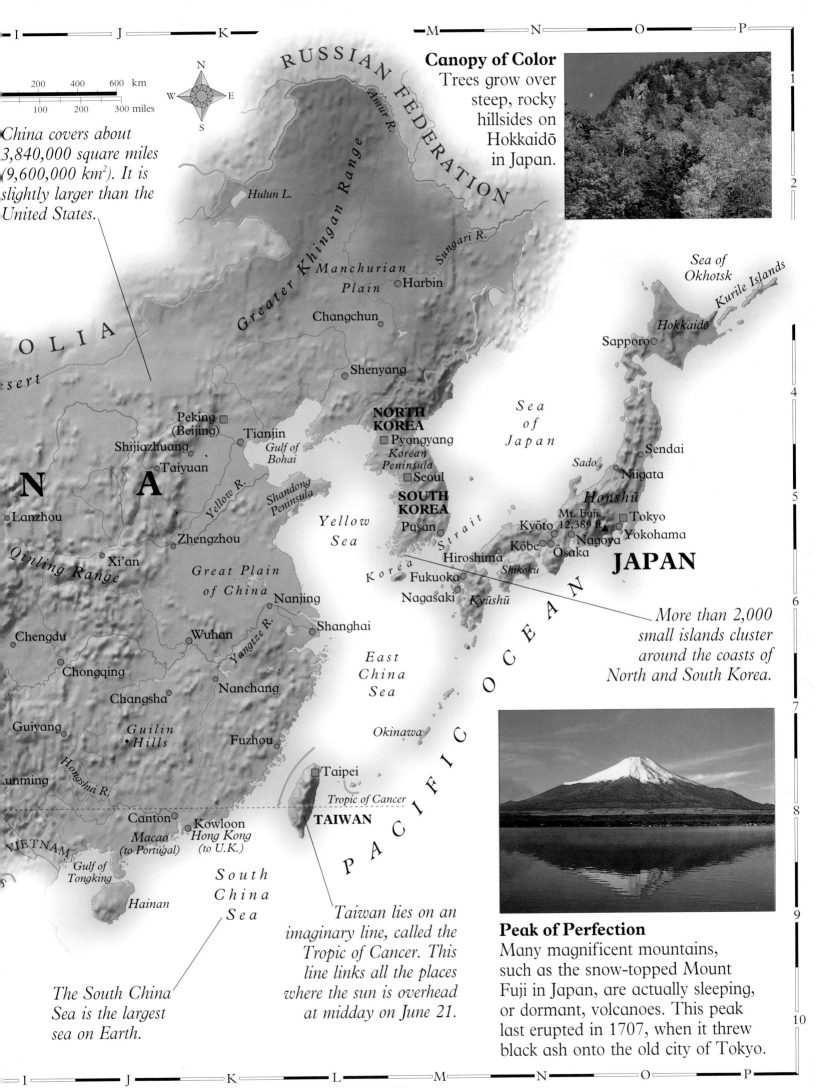

Canopy of Color
Trees grow over
steep, rocky
hillsides on
Hokkaidō
in Japan.

200 400 600 km

100 200 300 miles

*China covers about
3,840,000 square miles
(9,600,000 km²). It is
slightly larger than the
United States.*

RUSSIAN FEDERATION

*Sea of
Okhotsk*

Amur R.

Greater Khingan Range

Hulun L.

Kurile Islands

*Manchurian
Plain* •Harbin

Sungari R.

Hokkaidō

Changchun

Sapporo•

O L I A

Shenyang•

Sea
of
Japan

Sendai

**NORTH
KOREA**

□Pyongyang

Sado Niigata•

•Peking
(Beijing) □

Tianjin•

*Korean
Peninsula*

Honshū

N

Shijiazhuang•

*Gulf of
Bohai*

□Seoul

A

•Taiyuan

*Shandong
Peninsula*

**SOUTH
KOREA**

Mt. Fuji
12,389 ft ▲

□Tokyo

Lanzhou•

*Yellow
Sea*

Kyōto

•Yokohama

Yellow R.

Pusan•

*Korea
Strait*

Kōbe• Nagoya
•Osaka

Zhengzhou•

•Xi'an

Hiroshima•

JAPAN

Qinling Range

*Great Plain
of China*

Fukuoka•

Shikoku

•Nanjing

Nagasaki• *Kyūshū*

Chengdu•

Yangtze R.

•Shanghai

*More than 2,000
small islands cluster
around the coasts of
North and South Korea.*

•Wuhan

Chongqing•

*East
China
Sea*

Changsha•

•Nanchang

Guiyang•

*Guilin
•Hills*

Okinawa

Fuzhou•

Hongshui R.

unming•

•Taipei

Tropic of Cancer

Canton•

•Kowloon
*Hong Kong
(to U.K.)*

TAIWAN

*South
China
Sea*

*Macao
(to Portugal)*

P A C I F I C   O C E A N

VIETNAM

*Gulf of
Tongking*

Hainan

*Taiwan lies on an
imaginary line, called the
Tropic of Cancer. This
line links all the places
where the sun is overhead
at midday on June 21.*

*The South China
Sea is the largest
sea on Earth.*

Peak of Perfection
Many magnificent mountains,
such as the snow-topped Mount
Fuji in Japan, are actually sleeping,
or dormant, volcanoes. This peak
last erupted in 1707, when it threw
black ash onto the old city of Tokyo.

SOUTHEAST ASIA

The islands in southeast Asia form a chain that is about the same length as the distance across the United States. Cutting straight through the heart of this region there is an imaginary line, called the equator. Like most of the lands that lie on this line, southeast Asia is hot all year round. The warm, moist air forms rain clouds, and there are many thunderstorms. Tropical rain forests grow in this hot, humid climate.

Powerful winds, called typhoons, crash into the coast of Vietnam.

MYANMAR
Mandalay

Irrawaddy R.
Salween R.
Ping R.
Mekong R.
Red R.

BANGLADESH
INDIA
CHINA
Tropic of Cancer

LAOS
Louang Phrabang
Hanoi □
Hai Phong
Gulf of Tongking

Bay of Bengal

Chiang Mai
Vientiane □
Pegu
Rangoon □
Moulmein

THAILAND
Bangkok □

VIETNAM
Da Nang

CAMBODIA
L. Tônlé
Batdâmbâng

Andaman Islands (to India)
Port Blair

Andaman Sea

Gulf of Thailand

Phnom Penh
Ho Chi Minh City
Mekong Delta

Isthmus of Kra

Kakana

Nicobar Islands (to India)

Phuket I.
Ko Phi Phi I.
Nakhon Si Thammarat

Malay Peninsula

INDIAN

Pinang
MALAY

Medan
Strait of Malacca

Kuching

Sumatra

Kuala Lumpur □
SINGAPORE

Padang
Pontianak
Bangka I.

Palembang
IN

OCEAN

Krakatau I.

Jav
Jakarta
Semara
Bandung
Jav

N

One of Many
Ko Phi Phi Island lies off Thailand's coast. It is one of more than 20,000 islands that are packed into this region. Many of them were formed by volcanoes.

Colorful Mystery
Brightly colored lakes sit inside an extinct volcano on Flores Island. Nobody knows why, but sometimes the lakes suddenly change color. In the past, the waters have looked blue, rusty-brown, and black.

In 1883, the island of Krakatau was torn apart by one of the world's largest volcanic explosions.

Chocolate Galore

There are more than 1,000 peaks on the Philippine island of Bohol. They are called the Chocolate Hills because there is so little rain from February to May that the grass dries to a chocolate brown color.

Jungle Jamboree

Pitcher plant

Hibiscus

Stinking passionflower

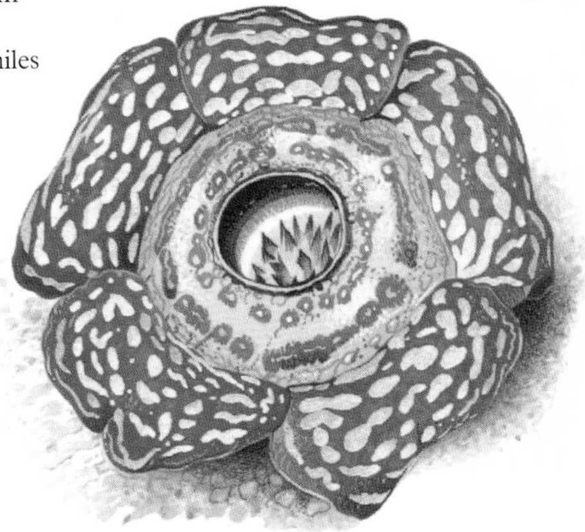

Rafflesia

Blowout

Mount Semeru in Java is a volcano – an opening that goes deep into the Earth. When a volcano erupts, it can hurl rocks and lava out high into the air.

The Earth's biggest cave is in Borneo. A 15-story building could fit inside it!

Irian Jaya in west New Guinea is a land of jungles, swamps, and high mountains.

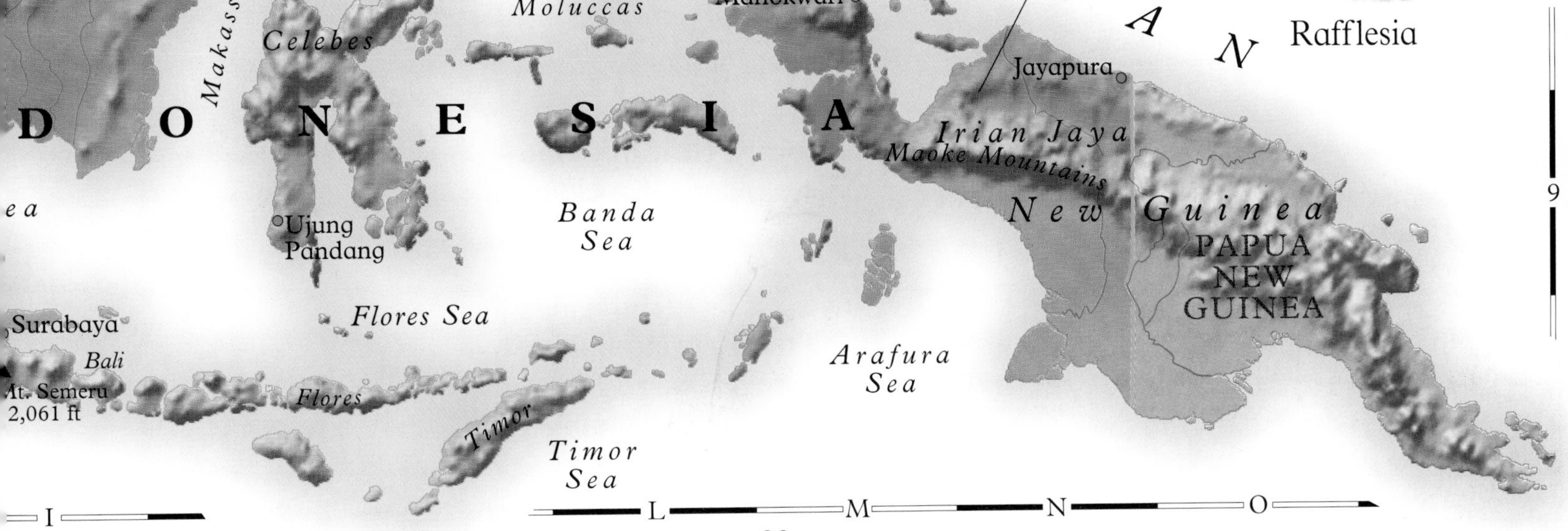

I J K L M N O P
1 2 3 4 5 6 9
Luzon
Dagupan
Manila
South China Sea
PHILIPPINES
Iloilo
Cebu
Bohol I.
Palawan I.
Mindanao
Davao
Zamboanga
Kota Kinabalu
Sulu Archipelago
Bandar Seri Begawan
BRUNEI
Celebes Sea
PACIFIC OCEAN
N
W
E
S
0 200 400 600 km
0 200 400 miles
Manado
Borneo
Makassar Strait
Equator
Manokwari
Moluccas
Celebes
Jayapura
INDONESIA
Irian Jaya
Maoke Mountains
New Guinea
PAPUA NEW GUINEA
Ujung Pandang
Banda Sea
Flores Sea
Surabaya
Bali
Mt. Semeru 2,061 ft
Flores
Timor
Timor Sea
Arafura Sea

AUSTRALIA

There are seven large landmasses, or continents, on Earth. Australia is the flattest and smallest of these continents, but it is still big enough for 23 countries the size of Italy to fit inside it! About two-thirds of Australia is covered by deserts and plains, known as the bush or outback. Rain falls on the coasts but rarely reaches the drier inland areas.

Rains and winds batter the north coast. In 1974, a cyclone blasted through Darwin.

Melville I.

INDIAN OCEAN

Timor Sea

Da.

Ar L

Wyndham

Broome

NOR

Tana Dese TER

Great Sandy Desert

Dampier

Hamersley Range

Tropic of Capricorn

Gibson Desert

WESTERN

AUST

Uluru (Ayers Rock) 2,848 ft

AUSTRALIA

Great Victoria Desert

A

Geraldton

Kalgoorlie

Nullarbor Plain

Perth

Fremantle

Great Australian Bi

Cape Leeuwin

Albany

Parts of Australia's 29,250-mile (47,070 km) coastline have sandy beaches.

Magical Hill
Rising suddenly from the desert floor, Ayers Rock seems to change color as the sun moves. It is sacred to the aboriginal people, who call it Uluru.

Shrinking Rock
These boulders in the Tanami Desert are shrinking. They expand in the hot midday sun and contract at night when it cools. Slowly, the outer layers crack and fall off.

Going, Going, Gone
These pillars of rock, or stacks, off the coast of Victoria were formed by waves. Powerful winds called the Roaring Forties caused waves to crash into the cliffs, which crumbled away, leaving these stacks.

Underwater Wilderness

Tiny underwater animals living together form the Great Barrier Reef – a coral reef that stretches for 1,430 miles (2,300 km). It is the largest living thing on Earth and is so big that astronauts have seen it from the moon!

Today, you can only find tropical rain forests in patches of northeast Australia, but scientists think jungles once covered the whole country.

rafura Sea

Torres Strait

Cape York

Gulf
of
Carpentaria

*Cape
York
Peninsula*

Cairns

Townsville

Mount Isa

Mackay

Flinders R.

QUEENSLAND

Great Barrier Reef

Great Dividing Range

PACIFIC OCEAN

ORY

Springs

RALIA

Diamantina R.

Rockhampton

Fraser I.

Charleville

Toowoomba

Brisbane

npson
esert

OUTH

L. Eyre

RALIA

L. Torrens

Flinders Ranges

irdner

Whyalla

NEW

Broken Hill

SOUTH

WALES

Maitland

Newcastle

Darling R.

Murray R.

Mildura

Murrumbidgee R.

Sydney

Wollongong

Adelaide

Wagga
Wagga

Canberra

Kangaroo I.

Mt. Kosciusko ▲
7,317 ft

AUSTRALIAN
CAPITAL
TERRITORY

VICTORIA

Geelong

Melbourne

Tasman Sea

King I.

Bass Strait
Flinders I.

Launceston

TASMANIA

The island state of Tasmania separated from the mainland about 25,000 years ago.

Hobart

N
W   E
S

0   100 200 300 400 500 km

0   100   200   300 miles

Amazing Australians

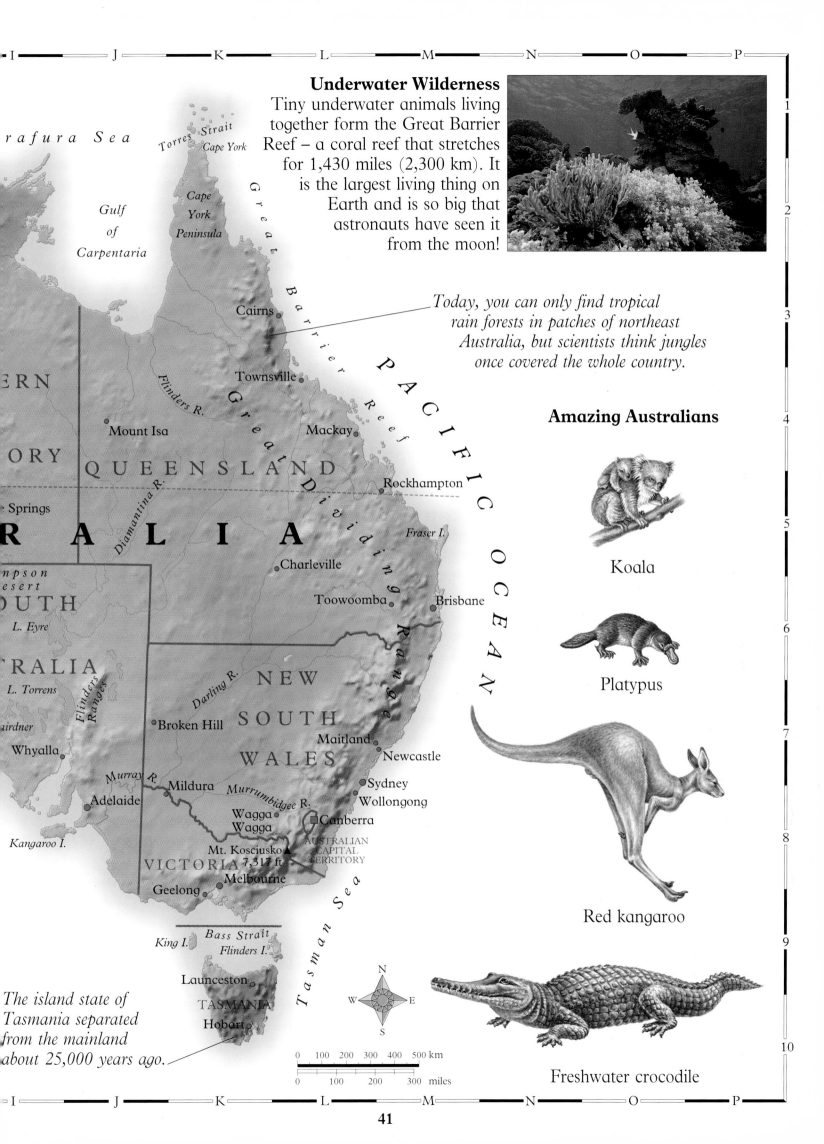

Koala

Platypus

Red kangaroo

Freshwater crocodile

New Zealand & the Pacific Islands

Tens of thousands of islands lie between the tropics in the vast waters of the warm Pacific Ocean. No one lives on most of them, and only 3,000 have names. New islands keep popping up as volcanoes erupt from the ocean floor. The weather in this tropical zone is hot and wet. However, places outside this area, such as New Zealand, are said to have a temperate climate because they are cooler.

Northern Mariana Islands
(to U.S.A.)

Saipan

Guam Agana
(to U.S.A.)

Koror

MI

PALAU

Equator

INDONESIA

New Guinea

Bismarck S.

Mt. Wilhelm
14,784 ft

PAPUA NEW GUINEA

Port Moresby

Coral Sea

Islands
(to Au

AUSTRALIA

Tropic of Capricorn

Underground Kettle
Beneath Rotorua in New Zealand, the ground is so hot that water boils. Steam builds up under the ground and explodes into a huge jet of hot water, called a geyser.

Great Balls of Stone
Each of these enormous balls of ancient rock weighs more than an elephant. No one knows how they reached this beach just north of Dunedin in New Zealand.

Emerald Forests
Rain forests need lots of rain to form. The hilly west coast of New Zealand's South Island is wet enough for thick, temperate rain forests to grow. They are carpeted in damp-loving mosses. The heavy rain is carried in by winds from the stormy Tasman Sea.

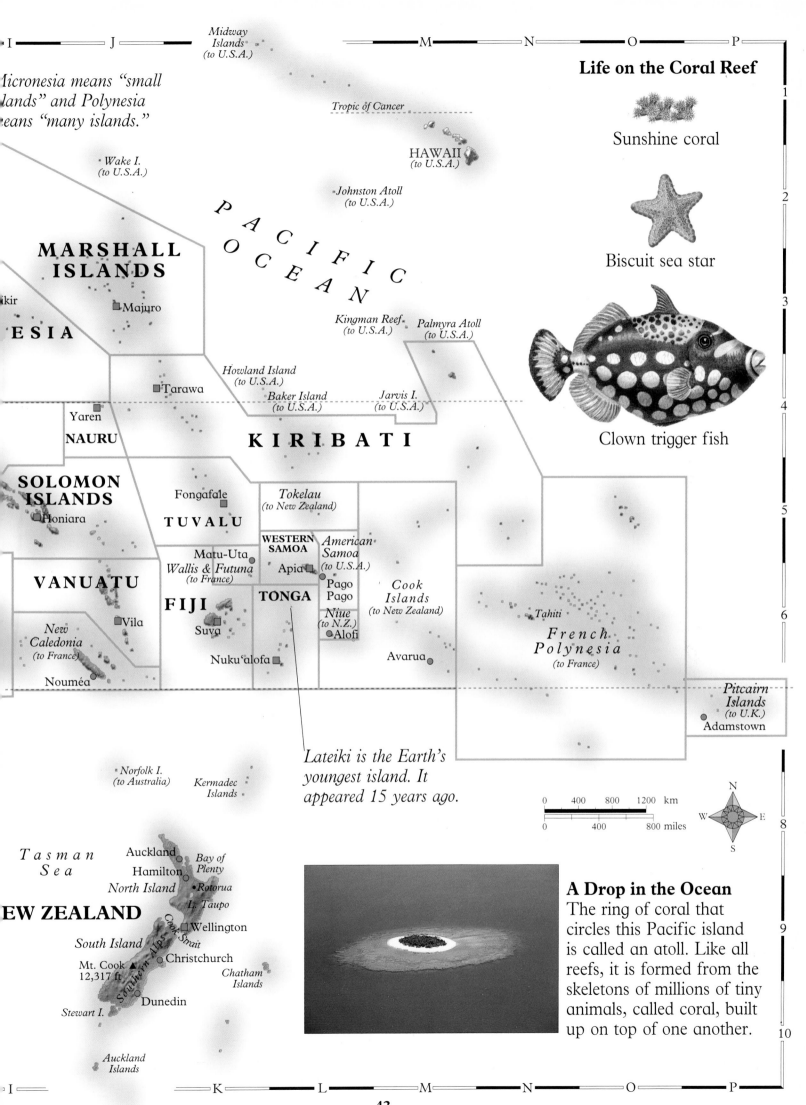

I   J   M   N   O   P

Midway Islands (to U.S.A.)

Life on the Coral Reef

Sunshine coral

Biscuit sea star

Micronesia means "small Islands" and Polynesia means "many islands."

Tropic of Cancer

HAWAII
(to U.S.A.)

Wake I. (to U.S.A.)

Johnston Atoll (to U.S.A.)

Clown trigger fish

MARSHALL ISLANDS

P A C I F I C

O C E A N

...ikir   ■Majuro

...ESIA

Kingman Reef (to U.S.A.)

Palmyra Atoll (to U.S.A.)

Howland Island (to U.S.A.)

■Tarawa

Baker Island (to U.S.A.)

Jarvis I. (to U.S.A.)

■Yaren

NAURU

K I R I B A T I

SOLOMON ISLANDS

Fongafale ■

Tokelau (to New Zealand)

□Honiara

TUVALU

WESTERN SAMOA

American Samoa (to U.S.A.)

Matu-Uta ■

Wallis & Futuna (to France)

Apia ■

VANUATU

FIJI

TONGA

Pago Pago

Cook Islands (to New Zealand)

Tahiti

■Vila

Suva ■

Niue (to N.Z.)
● Alofi

*F r e n c h
P o l y n e s i a
(to France)*

New Caledonia (to France)

Nuku'alofa ■

Avarua ●

Nouméa

Pitcairn Islands (to U.K.)
● Adamstown

Lateiki is the Earth's youngest island. It appeared 15 years ago.

Norfolk I. (to Australia)

Kermadec Islands

0   400   800   1200   km

0   400   800   miles

N
W   E
S

*T a s m a n
S e a*

Auckland ●

Bay of Plenty

Hamilton ●

North Island

● *Rotorua*

L. Taupo

A Drop in the Ocean

The ring of coral that circles this Pacific island is called an atoll. Like all reefs, it is formed from the skeletons of millions of tiny animals, called coral, built up on top of one another.

EW ZEALAND

□ Wellington

South Island

Cook Strait

Mt. Cook ▲ 12,317 ft

● Christchurch

Chatham Islands

● Dunedin

Stewart I.

Auckland Islands

I   K   L   M   N   O   P

43

INDEX

44

Côte d'Ivoire *Country* Africa 18 E8
Cozumel I. Mexico 15 J7
Crete *Island* Greece 28 G10
Croatia *Country* Europe 28 E8
Cuanza, R. Angola 20 G5
Cuba *Country* Caribbean Sea 15 L6
Cunene R. Angola/Namibia 20 G6
Curitiba Brazil 17 N6
Cyprus *Country* Mediterranean Sea 31 I4
Czech Republic *Country* Europe 27 L4

D

Da Nang Vietnam 38 H4
Dacca Bangladesh 35 N5
Dagupan Philippines 39 J4
Dakar Senegal 18 D7
Dallas U.S.A. 13 J7
Dampier Australia 40 E4
Danakil Depression Ethiopia 19 L7
Danube R. Europe 27 K4 & 28 G7
Dar es Salaam Tanzania 21 K4
Darien, Gulf of Colombia/Panama 15 L10 & 17 K1
Darling R. Australia 41 K7
Darwin Australia 40 H2
Davao Philippines 39 K6
Davis Strait Canada/Greenland 8 C8 & 11 M4
Dawson Canada 10 E5
Dead Sea *Lake* Israel/Jordan 31 J5
Death Valley U.S.A. 12 G6
Deccan Plateau India 35 J7
Delaware *State* U.S.A. 13 N6
Delgado, Cape Mozambique 21 K5
Denali (Mt. McKinley) *Mountain* U.S.A. 12 C7
Denmark *Country* Europe 23 J9
Denmark Strait Greenland/Iceland 9 E9
Denver U.S.A. 13 I5
Des Moines U.S.A. 13 K5
Detroit U.S.A. 13 M5
Devon I. Canada 11 K3
Diamantina, R. Australia 41 J5
Djibouti *Country* Africa 19 L7
Djibouti Djibouti 19 L8
Dnieper R. Europe 28 H7
Dodoma Tanzania 21 J4
Doha Qatar 31 M6
Dominica *Country* Caribbean Sea 15 P8
Dominican Republic *Country* Caribbean Sea 15 O7
Don R. Russian Federation 29 I7
Dordogne R. France 25 L7
Dortmund Germany 27 J3
Douro R. Portugal 25 I8
Drakensberg Mts. Lesotho/South Africa 21 I10
Drau R. Europe 27 L5
Dresden Germany 27 L3
Dubai United Arab Emirates 31 N6
Dubawnt, L. Canada 11 I5
Dublin Republic of Ireland 25 J4
Dunedin New Zealand 43 J10
Durban South Africa 21 J9
Dushanbe Tajikistan 32 E8
Düsseldorf Germany 27 I3
Dvina R., Northern Russian Federation 29 I1
Dvina R., Western Europe 28 G6

E

Easter I. *Chilean territory* Pacific Ocean 7 L8
Eastern Ghats *Mountains* India 35 K8
Eastmain R. Canada 11 L7
Ebro R. Spain 25 K8
Ecuador *Country* South America 17 J3
Edinburgh Scotland, U.K. 25 K3
Edmonton Canada 10 H7
Egypt *Country* Africa 19 J5
El Aaiún Western Sahara 18 D5
El Salvador *Country* North America 15 I9
Elba *Island* Italy 27 J7
Elbe R. Germany 27 K2
Elbrus, Mt. Russian Federation 29 I9
Elburz Mts. Iran 31 M3
Ellesmere I. Canada 8 D7 & 11 L2
Ellsworth Mts. Antarctica 9 K6
Ems R. Germany 27 J2

Enderby Land *Region* Antarctica 9 M5
England *Region* U.K. 25 K4
English Channel France/U.K. 25 K5
Equatorial Guinea *Country* Africa 20 F3
Erebus, Mt. Antarctica 9 L7
Erie, L. Canada/U.S.A. 11 K9 & 13 M5
Eritrea *Country* Africa 19 L7
Esbjerg Denmark 23 J10
Eşfahān Iran 31 M4
Essen Germany 27 I3
Estonia *Country* Europe 28 G5
Ethiopia *Country* Africa 19 K8
Ethiopian Highlands Ethiopia 19 K8
Etna *Mountain* Sicily, Italy 27 L9
Euphrates R. Asia 31 K4
Everest, Mt. China/Nepal 35 M4 & 36 F7
Everglades *Wetland* U.S.A. 13 M9
Eyre, L. Australia 41 I6

F

Faeroe Islands *Danish territory* Atlantic Ocean 22 E6
Faial *Island* Azores, Atlantic Ocean 24 D9
Fairbanks U.S.A. 12 D7
Faisalabad Pakistan 35 I3
Falcon L. Mexico/U.S.A. 14 G5
Falkland Islands *U.K. territory* Atlantic Ocean 17 M10
Farvel, Cape Greenland 9 C9
Fdérik Mauritania 18 D6
Fianarantsoa Madagascar 21 L7
Fiji *Country* Pacific Ocean 43 K6
Finland *Country* Europe 23 N3
Finland, Gulf of Europe 23 N7 & 28 G5
Fish R. Namibia 20 G8
Flinders I. Australia 41 K9
Flinders Ranges *Mountains* Australia 41 J7
Flinders R. Australia 41 J4
Florence Italy 27 K7
Flores *Island* Azores, Atlantic Ocean 24 D8
Flores *Island* Indonesia 39 J10
Florida *State* U.S.A. 13 M8
Florida, Straits of Cuba/U.S.A. 15 K6
Fongafale Tuvalu, Pacific Ocean 43 K5
Fort Peck, L. U.S.A. 12 H3
Fortaleza Brazil 17 O3
France *Country* Europe 25 K6
Frankfurt am Main Germany 27 J3
Franz Josef Land *Island group* Russian Federation 8 G7
Fraser R. Canada 10 G7
Fraser I. Australia 41 M5
Freetown Sierra Leone 18 D8
Fremantle Australia 40 E7
French Guiana *French territory* South America 17 M2
French Polynesia *French territory* Pacific Ocean 43 N6
Fria, Cape Namibia 20 F6
Fuerteventura *Island* Canary Islands, Atlantic Ocean 24 G9
Fuji, Mt. Japan 37 N5
Fukuoka Japan 37 M6
Fundy, Bay of Canada 11 M9
Fuzhou China 31 K7

G

Gabon *Country* Africa 20 F3
Gaborone Botswana 21 I8
Gairdner, L. Australia 41 I7
Galapagos Islands *Ecuadorian terrritory* Pacific Ocean 17 I3
Gambia *Country* Africa 18 C7
Ganges Delta Bangladesh 35 N6
Ganges R. Bangladesh/India 35 K4
Garda, L. Italy 27 K6
Garonne R. France 25 K7
Garry, L. Canada 11 J5
Gävle Sweden 23 M7
Gaziantep Turkey 31 J3
Gdańsk Poland 27 M1
Geelong Australia 41 K9
Geneva Switzerland 27 I5
Geneva, L. France/Switzerland 25 M6 & 27 I5
Genoa Italy 27 J6
Genoa, Gulf of Italy 27 J7
Georgetown Guyana 17 M1

Georgia *Country* Asia 29 I9
Georgia *State* U.S.A. 13 M7
Geraldton Australia 40 D6
Germany *Country* Europe 27 J3
Ghana *Country* Africa 18 F8
Giant's Causeway Northern Ireland, U.K. 25 I3
Gibraltar *U.K. territory* Mediterranean Sea 25 J10
Gibraltar, Strait of Morocco/Spain 25 J10
Gibson Desert Australia 40 G5
Giza Egypt 19 K4
Glåna R. Norway 23 K6
Glasgow Scotland, U.K. 25 J3
Gobi Desert China/Mongolia 32 H8 & 36 H4
Godavari R. India 35 K7
Godthåb Greenland 9 C9
Golan Heights *Disputed territory* Syria 31 J4
Good Hope, Cape of South Africa 20 H10
Göteborg Sweden 23 K8
Gotland *Island* Sweden 23 M8
Grampian Mts. Scotland, U.K. 25 J2
Gran Canaria *Island* Canary Islands, Atlantic Ocean 24 G9
Grand Bahama I. Bahamas 15 K5
Grand Canyon U.S.A. 12 G6
Grande, Rio Mexico/U.S.A. 13 I7 & 14 G4
Graz Austria 27 L5
Great Abaco I. Bahamas 15 L5
Great Australian Bight *Bay* Australia 40 H7
Great Bahama Bank *Sea feature* Caribbean Sea 15 L6
Great Bahama I. Bahamas 15 K5
Great Barrier Reef Australia 41 K2
Great Basin U.S.A. 12 F5
Great Bear L. Canada 10 G5
Great Dividing Range *Mountains* Austalia 41 K4
Great Lakes Canada/U.S.A. 11 K8 & 13 L4
Great Plain of China China 37 K6
Great Plains U.S.A. 13 I4
Great Rift Valley Africa/Asia 20 I3
Great Salt Desert Iran 31 M4
Great Salt L. U.S.A. 12 G5
Great Sandy Desert Australia 40 F4
Great Slave L. Canada 10 H5
Great Victoria Desert Australia 40 F6
Greater Antilles *Island group* Caribbean Sea 15 K7
Greater Khingan Range *Mountains* China 37 K3
Greece *Country* Europe 28 F9
Greenland *Danish territory* Atlantic Ocean 8 D8
Grenada *Country* Caribbean Sea 15 P9
Grotte de Clamouse *Cave* France 25 I7
Guadalajara Mexico 14 G7
Guadalquivir R. Spain 25 J10
Guadalupe I. Mexico 14 D4
Guadeloupe *French territory* Caribbean Sea 15 P8
Guadiana R. Portugal/Spain 25 J9
Guam *U.S.A. territory* Pacific Ocean 42 G2
Guatemala *Country* North America 15 I8
Guatemala City Guatemala 15 I8
Guayaquil Ecuador 17 J3
Guiana Highlands South America 17 L2
Guilin Hills China 37 J7
Guinea *Country* Africa 18 D8
Guinea, Gulf of Africa 18 F9
Guinea-Bissau *Country* Africa 18 C8
Guiyang China 37 I7
Guyana *Country* South America 17 M1

H

Hague, The Netherlands 25 M4
Hai Phong Vietnam 38 H3
Hainan *Island* China 37 J9
Haiti *Country* Caribbean Sea 15 M7
Ḩalab Syria 31 J3
Halifax Canada 11 M9
Hamburg Germany 27 K2
Hamersley Range *Mountains* Australia 40 D4

Hamilton New Zealand 43 K8
Hamilton Canada 11 L9
Hanoi Vietnam 38 G3
Hanover Germany 27 J2
Harare Zimbabwe 21 J6
Harbin China 37 M3
Hardanger Fjord Norway 23 I7
Hargeysa Somalia 19 L8
Havana Cuba 15 K6
Hawaii *Island* Hawaii, Pacific Ocean 12 D10
Hawaii *State* U.S.A. 12 C10
Helena U.S.A. 12 H3
Helsinki Finland 23 O7
Herāt Afghanistan 32 E9
Himalayas *Mountains* China/India/Nepal 35 J2 & 36 E6
Hindu Kush *Mountains* Afghanistan 32 E9
Hiroshima Japan 37 N6
Ho Chi Minh City Vietnam 38 H5
Hobart Australia 41 K10
Hokkaidō *Island* Japan 37 O3
Holguín Cuba 15 L7
Honduras *Country* North America 15 J8
Honduras, Gulf of North America 15 J8
Hong Kong *U.K. territory* Asia 37 K8
Hongshui R. China 37 I8
Honiara Solomon Islands 43 I5
Honolulu Oahu I. Hawaii, Pacific Ocean 12 D9
Honshū *Island* Japan 37 O5
Hormuz, Strait of Iran/Oman 31 N6
Horn, Cape Chile 17 L10
Houston U.S.A. 13 K8
Howland I. *U.S.A. territory* Pacific Ocean 43 K4
Huambo Angola 20 G6
Hudson R. U.S.A. 13 N5
Hudson Bay Canada 11 K6
Hudson Strait Canada 11 L5
Hulun L. China 37 K2
Hungary *Country* Europe 28 F8
Huron, L. Canada/U.S.A. 11 K8 & 13 M4
Hyderabad India 35 K7
Hyderabad Pakistan 34 H5

I

Iberian Peninsula Europe 25 J9
Iceland *Country* Atlantic Ocean 22 D6
Idaho *State* U.S.A. 12 G4
Illinois *State* U.S.A. 13 L5
Iloilo Philippines 39 J5
Inari, L. Finland 23 N2
India *Country* Asia 35 I5
Indiana *State* U.S.A. 13 L5
Indonesia *Country* Asia 38 G9
Indus R. Asia 34 H5 & 35 I3
Inn R. Europe 27 K4
Inner Hebrides *Islands* Scotland, U.K. 25 J2
Innsbruck Austria 27 K5
Iowa *State* U.S.A. 13 K5
Iran *Country* Asia 31 M4
Iran, Plateau of Iran 31 M4
Iraq *Country* Asia 31 K5
Ireland, Republic of *Country* Europe 25 I3
Irian Jaya *Region* Indonesia 39 M9
Irkutsk Russian Federation 32 H6
Irrawaddy R. Myanmar 38 E3
Irtysh, R. Asia 32 E5
Islamabad Pakistan 35 I2
Israel *Country* Asia 31 I4
Issyk-kul', L. Kyrgyzstan 32 F8
Istanbul Turkey 30 H2
Italy *Country* Europe 27 K6
Izmir Turkey 30 H3

J

Jabalpur India 35 K5
Jackson U.S.A. 13 L7
Jaffna Sri Lanka 35 K10
Jaipur India 35 J4
Jakarta Indonesia 38 H9
Jamaica *Country* Caribbean Sea 15 L7
James Bay Canada 11 K7

New Caledonia *French territory* Pacific Ocean 43 I6
New Delhi India 35 J4
New Guinea *Island* Indonesia/Papua New Guinea 39 N9, 42 G4
New Hampshire *State* U.S.A. 13 O4
New Jersey *State* U.S.A. 13 N5
New Mexico *State* U.S.A. 13 I7
New Orleans U.S.A. 13 L8
New Siberian Islands Russian Federation 8 G5 & 33 L3
New South Wales *State* Australia 41 K6
New York *State* U.S.A. 13 N4
New York U.S.A. 13 O5
New Zealand *Country* Pacific Ocean 43 I9
Newcastle Australia 41 M7
Newcastle upon Tyne England, U.K. 25 K3
Newfoundland *Island* Canada 11 N8
Newfoundland *Province* Canada 11 M6
Niagara Falls *Waterfall* Canada/U.S.A. 11 L9 & 13 N5
Niamey Niger 18 F7
Nicaragua *Country* North America 15 J9
Nicaragua, L. Nicaragua 15 K9
Nice France 25 M7
Nicobar Islands *Indian territory* Indian Ocean 38 E6
Nicosia Cyprus 31 I4
Niger *Country* Africa 18 G6
Niger R. Africa 18 G8
Nigeria *Country* Africa 18 G8
Niigata Japan 37 O5
Nile Delta Egypt 19 J4
Nile R. Africa 19 K6
Nipigon, L. Canada 11 K8
Niue *New Zealand territory* Pacific Ocean 43 L6
Nizhniy Novgorod Russian Federation 29 J6
Norfolk I. *Australian territory* Pacific Ocean 43 J7
Norrköping Sweden 23 L8
North Cape Norway 23 N1
North Carolina *State* U.S.A. 13 N6
North Dakota *State* U.S.A. 13 I3
North European Plain Europe 27 K2 & 28 H6
North Island New Zealand 43 J9
North Korea *Country* Asia 37 L4
North Pole Arctic Ocean 8 F7
Northern Ireland *Region* U.K. 25 J3
Northern Mariana Islands *U.S.A. territory* Pacific Ocean 42 H2
Northern Territory Australia 40 H4
Northwest Territories *Province* Canada 10 G4
Norway *Country* Europe 23 J7
Nouakchott Mauritania 18 D6
Nouméa New Caledonia, Pacific Ocean 43 J7
Nova Scotia *Province* Canada 11 M9
Novaya Zemlya *Island group* Russian Federation 29 K1
Novosibirsk Russian Federation 32 F6
Nubian Desert Sudan 19 K6
Nuku'alofa Tonga, Pacific Ocean 43 L6
Nullarbor Plain Australia 40 G7
Nuremberg Germany 27 K4
Nyasa, L. Africa 21 J5

O

Oahe, L. U.S.A. 13 J4
Oahu *Island* Hawaii State, Pacific Ocean 12 D9
Ob' R. Russian Federation 32 E4
Odense Denmark 23 J10
Oder R. Germany 27 L2
Odesa Ukraine 28 H8
Odra R. Poland 27 M3
Ohio *State* U.S.A. 13 M5
Ohio R. U.S.A. 13 L6
Okavango Delta Botswana 20 H7
Okavango R. Africa 20 G6
Okeechobee, L. U.S.A. 13 M8
Okinawa *Island* Japan 37 L7
Oklahoma *State* U.S.A. 13 J7
Oklahoma City U.S.A. 13 J6
Öland *Island* Sweden 23 M9
Omaha U.S.A. 13 K5
Oman *Country* Asia 31 N8

Oman, Gulf of Iran/Oman 31 N7
Omdurman Sudan 19 K7
Omsk Russian Federation 32 F6
Onega, L. Russian Federation 28 H4
Ontario *Province* Canada 11 J7
Ontario, L. Canada/U.S.A. 11 L9 & 13 N4
Oran Algeria 18 F3
Orange R. Africa 20 H9
Oregon *State* U.S.A. 12 F5
Orinoco R. Venezuela 17 L2
Orkney Islands U.K. 25 K1
Orléans France 25 L6
Ōsaka Japan 37 N5
Osh Kyrgyzstan 32 F8
Oslo Norway 23 K7
Östersund Sweden 23 L6
Ostrava Czech Republic 27 M4
Ottawa Canada 11 L8
Ottawa R. Canada 11 L8
Ouagadougou Burkina 18 F7
Oulu Finland 23 N4
Oulu, L. Finland 23 O5
Outer Hebrides *Island group* U.K. 25 I2

P

Padang Indonesia 38 F8
Pago Pago American Samoa, Pacific Ocean 43 L6
Paine Horns Chile 17 K10
Pakistan *Country* Asia 34 G4
Palau *Country* Pacific Ocean 42 G3
Palawan I. Philippines 39 J5
Palembang Indonesia 38 G9
Palermo Sicily, Italy 27 L9
Palikir Micronesia 43 I3
Palmyra Atoll *U.S.A. territory* Pacific Ocean 43 M3
Pampas *Region* Argentina 17 L7
Pamukkale Turkey 30 H3
Panama *Country* North America 15 K10
Panama Canal Panama 15 K10
Panama City Panama 15 L10
Panama, Gulf of Panama 15 L10
Panuco R. Mexico 14 G6
Papua New Guinea *Country* Pacific Ocean 42 H5
Paraguay *Country* South America 17 L5
Paraguay R. South America 17 M5
Paramaribo Suriname 17 M2
Paraná R. Argentina/Paraguay 17 M6
Paris France 25 L5
Patagonia *Region* Argentina 17 K10
Patna India 35 L5
Peace R. Canada 10 G6
Pechora R. Russian Federation 29 K3
Pecos R. U.S.A. 13 I7
Pegu Myanmar 38 E4
Peking (Beijing) China 37 K4
Pennsylvania *State* U.S.A. 13 M5
Persian Gulf Middle East 31 M5
Perth Australia 40 E7
Peru *Country* South America 17 K3
Peshawar Pakistan 35 I2
Peter 1st I. *Norwegian territory* Antarctica 9 I6
Petropavlovsk-Kamchatskiy Russian Federation 33 M6
Philadelphia U.S.A. 13 N5
Philippine Trench Pacific Ocean 4 G5
Philippines *Country* Asia 39 J5
Phnom Penh Cambodia 38 G5
Phoenix U.S.A. 12 H7
Phuket I. Thailand 38 E6
Pico *Island* Azores, Atlantic Ocean 24 E9
Pierre U.S.A. 13 J4
Pinang Malaysia 38 F6
Pines, Isle of *Island* Cuba 15 K7
Ping R. Thailand 38 F3
Pitcairn Islands *U.K. territory* Pacific Ocean 43 P7
Pittsburgh U.S.A. 13 M5
Plate R. Argentina/Uruguay 17 M7
Plenty, Bay of New Zealand 43 K8
Po, R. Italy 27 J6
Pointe-Noire Congo 20 G4
Poland *Country* Europe 27 M3
Ponta Delgada São Miguel Azores, Atlantic Ocean 24 E9
Pontianak Indonesia 38 H8
Poopó, L. Bolivia 17 L5
Popocatépetl *Mountain* Mexico 14 H7

Port-au-Prince Haiti 15 M7
Port Blair Andaman Islands, Indian Ocean 38 E5
Port Elizabeth South Africa 21 I10
Port-Gentil Gabon 20 F3
Port Louis Mauritius 21 N7
Port Moresby Papua New Guinea 42 H5
Port of Spain Trinidad & Tobago 15 P9
Port Said Egypt 19 K4
Port Sudan Sudan 19 K6
Portland U.S.A. 12 F4
Porto Portugal 25 I8
Pôrto Alegre Brazil 17 N6
Porto-Novo Benin 18 G8
Porto Santo *Island* Madeira Islands, Atlantic Ocean 24 G8
Portugal *Country* Europe 25 I9
Poznań Poland 27 M2
Prague Czech Republic 27 L3
Praia Cape Verde, Atlantic Ocean 18 C7
Prairies *Region* Canada/U.S.A. 10 H7 & 13 I3
Pretoria South Africa 21 I8
Prince Edward Island *Province* Canada 11 M8
Prince of Wales I. Canada 11 I3
Pripet R. Belarus/Ukraine 28 G7
Pripet Marshes *Wetlands* Belarus 28 G7
Puebla Mexico 14 H7
Puerto Rico *U.S.A. territory* Caribbean Sea 15 N8
Pune India 35 I7
Punta Arenas Chile 17 K10
Pusan South Korea 37 M5
Pyongyang North Korea 37 M4
Pyramid, L. U.S.A. 12 F5
Pyrenees *Mountains* Europe 25 K8

Q

Qaidam Basin China 36 G5
Qandahār Afghanistan 32 E9
Qatar *Country* Asia 31 M7
Qattâra Depression Egypt 19 J4
Qilian Mts. China 36 H4
Qinghai L. China 36 H5
Qinling Range *Mountains* China 37 I6
Qom Iran 31 M4
Quebec Canada 11 M8
Quebec *Province* Canada 11 L7
Queen Charlotte Islands Canada 10 F7
Queen Elizabeth Islands Canada 8 D6 & 10 H2
Queen Maud Land *Region* Antarctica 9 L5
Queensland *State* Australia 41 J5
Quetta Pakistan 34 H3
Quito Ecuador 17 K2

R

Rabat Morocco 18 E3
Raleigh U.S.A. 13 N6
Rangoon Myanmar 38 E4
Rawalpindi Pakistan 35 I2
Recife Brazil 17 O3
Red R. U.S.A. 13 J7
Red R. Vietnam 38 G2
Reindeer L. Canada 11 I6
Réunion I. *French territory* Indian Ocean 21 N7
Reykjavik Iceland 22 D6
Rhine Gorge Germany 27 J3
Rhine R. Europe 27 I3
Rhode Island *State* U.S.A. 13 O5
Rhône R. France/Switzerland 25 M7 & 27 J5
Richmond U.S.A. 13 N6
Riga Latvia 28 G5
Rio de Janeiro Brazil 17 N5
Riyadh Saudi Arabia 31 L7
Rockhampton Australia 41 M5
Rocky Mountains Canada/USA 10 E6 & 12 G3
Romania *Country* Europe 28 G8
Rome Italy 27 K7
Ronne Ice Shelf Antarctica 9 K5
Ross Ice Shelf Antarctica 9 L7
Rotorua New Zealand 43 K9
Rotterdam Netherlands 25 M4
Rub' al Khali *Desert* Saudi Arabia 31 L8

Russian Federation *Country* Asia/Europe 28 F6, 29 I5 & 32 D5
Rwanda *Country* Africa 21 I3
Rybinsk Reservoir Russian Federation 29 I5

S

Sable, Cape Canada 11 M9
Sado *Island* Japan 37 N5
Sahara Desert Africa 18 F5
Sahel *Region* Africa 18 E7
Saimaa, L. Finland 23 O6
St. Helens, Mt. U.S.A. 12 F4
St. John's Canada 11 O8
St. Kitts & Nevis *Country* Caribbean Sea 15 O8
St. Lawrence, Gulf of Canada 11 M8
St. Lawrence R. Canada 11 L8
St. Louis U.S.A. 13 L6
St. Lucia *Country* Caribbean Sea 15 O9
St. Petersburg Russian Federation 28 H5
St. Pierre & Miquelon *French territory* Canada 11 N8
St. Vincent and the Grenadines *Country* Caribbean Sea 15 O9
Saipan Northern Mariana Islands, Pacific Ocean 42 H2
Sakakawea, L. U.S.A. 13 I3
Sakhalin I. Russian Federation 33 L6
Salado R. Argentina 17 L7
Salar de Uyuni, L. Bolivia 17 L5
Salinas Grandes, L. Argentina 17 L6
Salt Lake City U.S.A. 12 H5
Salton Sea *Lake* U.S.A. 12 G7
Salvador Brazil 17 O4
Salween R. China/Myanmar 36 G6 & 38 F3
Salzburg Austria 27 L5
Samara Russian Federation 29 K6
Samaria Gorge Crete, Greece 28 G10
Samarkand Uzbekistan 32 E8
San Andreas Fault U.S.A. 12 F6
San Antonio U.S.A. 13 J8
San Diego U.S.A. 12 G7
San Francisco U.S.A. 12 F6
San Jorge *Gulf* Argentina 17 L9
San José Costa Rica 15 K10
San Juan Puerto Rico 15 O7
San Marino *Country* Europe 27 K6
San Matías *Gulf* Argentina 17 L8
San Salvador El Salvador 15 J9
San'ā Yemen 31 K9
Santa Fe Argentina 17 M7
Santa Fe U.S.A. 13 I6
Santiago Chile 17 K7
Santiago de Cuba Cuba 15 L7
Santo Domingo Dominican Republic 15 N7
São Francisco R. Brazil 17 N4
São Miguel *Island* Azores, Atlantic Ocean 24 E9
São Paulo Brazil 17 N6
São Roque *Cape* Brazil 17 O3
São Tomé Sao Tome & Principe 20 F3
Sao Tome & Principe *Country* Africa 20 E3
Saône R. France 25 M6
Sapporo Japan 37 O4
Sarajevo Bosnia-Herzegovina 28 F8
Sardinia *Italian territory* Mediterranean Sea 27 J8
Sarh Chad 19 I8
Saskatchewan *Province* Canada 11 I7
Saskatchewan R., North Canada 10 G7
Saudi Arabia *Country* Asia 31 K7
Scotland *Region* U.K. 25 J2
Scott Base *Research Station* Antarctica 9 L7
Seattle U.S.A. 12 F3
Seine R. France 25 L5
Semarang Indonesia 38 H10
Semeru, Mt. Indonesia 39 I10
Sendai Japan 37 O5
Senegal *Country* Africa 18 D7
Senegal R. Africa 18 D7
Seoul South Korea 37 M5
Severn, R. England, U.K. 25 K4
Severnaya Zemlya *Island group* Russian Federation 8 G6 & 32 G2
Sevilla Spain 25 J10
Seychelles *Country* Indian Ocean 21 L5

Sfax Tunisia 18 H3
Shandong Peninsula China 37 K5
Shanghai China 37 L6
Shannon R. Republic of Ireland 25 I4
Shebeli R. Ethiopia/Somalia 19 L8
Sheffield England, U.K. 25 K4
Shenyang China 37 L4
Shetland Islands Scotland, U.K. 25 K1
Shijiazhuang China 37 K5
Shikoku *Island* Japan 37 N6
Shīrāz Iran 31 M5
Siberia Russian Federation 32 G5
Sicily *Island* Italy 27 L10
Sierra de Loarre *Mountains* Spain 25 K8
Sierra Leone *Country* Africa 18 D8
Sierra Madre *Mountains* Guatemala/Mexico 14 F5
Sierra Morena *Mountains* Spain 25 J10
Sierra Nevada *Mountains* Spain 25 K10
Sierra Nevada *Mountains* U.S.A. 12 F5 & 25 K10
Sigirya Sri Lanka 35 K10
Silesian Plateau Poland 27 N3
Simpson Desert Australia 41 I5
Singapore *Country* Asia 38 G8
Sirte, Gulf of Libya 19 I4
Sīstān, L. Iran 31 O5
Sjaelland *Island* Denmark 23 K10
Skopje Macedonia 28 F9
Skovorodno Russian Federation 33 J6
Slovakia *Country* Europe 27 M4
Slovenia *Country* Europe 28 E8
Snake R. U.S.A. 12 G5
Socotra *Island* Yemen 31 M10
Sofia Bulgaria 28 G9
Sogne Fjord Norway 23 I6
Solomon Islands *Country* Pacific Ocean 43 I5
Somalia *Country* Africa 19 L9
Somerset I. Canada 10 J3
Sonoran Desert Mexico/U.S.A. 12 G7, 14 E4
South Africa *Country* Africa 20 H8
South Australia *State* Australia 41 I6
South Carolina *State* U.S.A. 13 M7
South Dakota *State* U.S.A. 13 I4
South Island New Zealand 43 J9
South Korea *Country* Asia 37 M5
South Orkney Islands *U.K. territory* Southern Ocean 9 J4
South Polar Plateau Antarctica 9 L6
South Pole Antarctica 9 L6
South Shetland Islands *U.K. territory* Southern Ocean 9 I4
Southampton I. Canada 11 K5
Southern Alps *Mountains* New Zealand 43 J10
Spain *Country* Europe 25 J8
Sri Lanka *Country* Asia 35 K10
Stanovoy Range *Mountains* Russian Federation 33 J6
Stavanger Norway 23 I8
Stewart I. New Zealand 43 J10
Stockholm Sweden 23 M8
Stor, L. Sweden 23 L5
Strasbourg France 25 N5
Streymoy I. Faeroe Islands, Atlantic Ocean 22 F6
Stuttgart Germany 27 J4
Sudan *Country* Africa 19 J7
Sudd Sudan 19 K8
Sulu Archipelago *Island group* Philippines 39 K6
Sumatra *Island* Indonesia 38 F7
Sungari R. China/Russian Federation 37 M3
Superior, L. Canada/U.S.A. 11 J8 & 13 L3
Surabaya Indonesia 39 I10
Suriname *Country* South America 17 M1
Surtsey I. Iceland 22 D6
Suva Fiji 43 K6
Svalbard *Norwegian territory* Arctic Ocean 8 F8
Sverdrup Islands Canada 11 I2
Swaziland *Country* Africa 21 J8
Sweden *Country* Europe 23 L7
Switzerland *Country* Europe 27 I5
Sydney Australia 41 L7
Syria *Country* Asia 31 J4
Syrian Desert Asia 31 J4
Szczecin Poland 27 L2

T

Table Mt. South Africa 20 H10
Tabrīz Iran 31 L2
Tagus R. Portugal/Spain 25 K9
Tahiti *Island* French Polynesia, Pacific Ocean 43 N6
Taipei Taiwan 37 L8
Taiwan *Country* Asia 37 L8
Taiyuan China 37 J5
Ta'izz Yemen 31 K10
Tajikistan *Country* Asia 32 E8
Taklamakan Desert China 36 E4
Tallinn Estonia 28 G5
Tamanrasset Oasis Algeria 18 G6
Tampa U.S.A. 13 M8
Tampere Finland 23 N6
Tana, L. Ethiopia 19 L7
Tana R. Norway 23 N2
Tanami Desert Australia 40 H4
Tanganyika, L. Africa 21 I4
Tangier Morocco 18 E3
Tanzania *Country* Africa 21 I4
Tapajós R. Brazil 17 M4
Taranto Italy 27 M8
Taranto, Gulf of Italy 27 M8
Tarawa Kiribati, Pacific Ocean 43 J4
Tarim R. China 36 E4
Tashkent Uzbekistan 32 E8
Tasmania *State* Australia 41 K10
Taupo, L. New Zealand 43 K9
Taurus Mts. Turkey 31 H3
Taymyr Peninsula Russian Federation 33 I3
Tbilisi Georgia 29 J9
Tegucigalpa Honduras 15 J9
Tehran Iran 31 M3
Tel Aviv Israel 31 I4
Tenerife *Island* Canary Islands, Atlantic Ocean 24 F9
Tennessee *State* U.S.A. 13 L6
Tennessee R. U.S.A. 13 L7
Terceira *Island* Azores, Atlantic Ocean 24 E8
Texas *State* U.S.A. 13 J7
Thailand *Country* Asia 38 F4
Thailand, Gulf of Thailand 38 F5
Thames, R. England, U.K. 25 K4
Thar Desert India/Pakistan 35 I4
Thessaloniki Greece 28 G9
Thimphu Bhutan 35 N4
Thule Greenland 8 D7
Tianjin China 37 K4
Tiber R. Italy 27 K7
Tibesti Mountains Chad/Libya 19 I6
Tibet *Region* China 36 F6
Tibet, Plateau of China 36 F6
Tien Shan Mts. China/Kyrgyzstan 36 E4
Tigris R. Asia 31 K4
Tijuana Mexico 14 D4
Timbuktu Mali 18 F7
Timor *Island* Indonesia 39 L10
Tirana Albania 28 F9
Titicaca, L. Bolivia/Peru 17 L4
Tobakakar Hills *Mountains* Afghanistan/Pakistan 34 I4
Tocantins R. Brazil 17 N4
Togo *Country* Africa 18 F8
Tokelau *New Zealand territory* Pacific Ocean 43 L5
Tokyo Japan 37 O5
Tomsk Russian Federation 32 G6
Tonga *Country* Pacific Ocean 43 K6
Tonga Trench Pacific Ocean 5 J7
Tongking, Gulf of China/Vietnam 37 J9 & 38 H3
Tônlé, L. Cambodia 38 G5
Toowoomba Australia 41 M6
Topeka U.S.A. 13 K5
Torne R. Sweden 23 N3
Toronto Canada 11 L9
Torrens, L. Australia 41 I7
Torreón Mexico 14 G5
Torres Strait Australia/Papua New Guinea 41 J1
Tórshavn Streymoy I. Faeroe Islands, Atlantic Ocean 22 F6
Toulouse France 25 L7
Townsville Australia 41 L4
Transantarctic Mountains Antarctica 9 L5
Transylvanian Alps *Mountains* Romania 28 G7
Trieste Italy 27 L6
Trinidad & Tobago *Country* Caribbean Sea 15 P9

Tripoli Libya 18 H4
Tromelin I. *French territory* Indian Ocean 21 M6
Tromsø Norway 23 M2
Trondheim Norway 23 K5
Tunis Tunisia 18 H3
Tunisia *Country* Africa 18 G3
Turin Italy 27 J6
Turkana, L. Ethiopia/Kenya 19 K9 & 21 J2
Turkey *Country* Asia 31 I2
Turkmenistan *Country* Asia 32 D8
Turks & Caicos Islands *U.K. territory* Caribbean Sea 15 M6
Turku Finland 23 N7
Tuvalu *Country* Pacific Ocean 43 K5
Tuz, L. Turkey 31 I3
Tyrol *Mountains* Austria 27 K5

U

Ubangi R. Central African Republic/Congo 20 G3
Uele R. Central African Republic/Zaire 21 I2
Uganda *Country* Africa 21 J2
Ujung Pandang Indonesia 39 J9
Ukraine *Country* Europe 28 G7
Ulan Bator Mongolia 33 I7
Ulan-Ude Russian Federation 33 I6
Uliastay Mongolia 32 H7
Uluru (Ayers Rock) *Mountain* Australia 40 H5
Ume R. Sweden 23 M5
Ungava Bay Canada 11 M6
Ungava Peninsula Canada 11 L6
United Arab Emirates *Country* Asia 31 M7
United Kingdom *Country* Europe 25 K3
United States of America *Country* North America 12-13
Uppsala Sweden 23 M7
Ural Mountains Russian Federation 29 L5 & 32 E5
Ural'sk Kazakhstan 32 D7
Urmia, L. Iran 31 L3
Uruguay *Country* South America 17 M7
Ürümqi China 36 F3
Utah *State* U.S.A. 12 G6
Utrecht Netherlands 25 M4
Uzbekistan *Country* Asia 32 D8

V

Vaasa Finland 23 N5
Vadsø Norway 23 O1
Valencia Spain 25 K9
Valladolid Spain 25 J8
Valletta Malta 27 L10
Van, L. Turkey 31 K2
Vancouver Canada 10 G8
Vancouver I. Canada 10 F8
Väner, L. Sweden 23 K8
Vanuatu *Country* Pacific Ocean 43 I6
Varanger Fjord Norway 23 O1
Västerås Sweden 23 L7
Vatican City *Country* Rome, Italy 27 K7
Vatnajökull Ice Sheet Iceland 22 D6
Vätter, L. Sweden 23 L8
Vaygach I. Russian Federation 29 L2
Venezuela *Country* South America 17 K1
Venice Italy 27 K6
Verkhoyansk Range *Mountains* Russian Federation 33 J4
Vermont *State* U.S.A. 13 O4
Verona *State* Australia 41 J8
Victoria I. Canada 10 G4
Victoria Falls *Waterfall* Zambia/Zimbabwe 21 I6
Victoria I. Canada 10 G4
Victoria, L. Africa 21 J3
Victoria Land *Region* Antarctica 9 L7
Vienna Austria 27 M4
Vientiane Laos 38 G3
Vietnam *Country* Asia 38 H4
Vila Vanuatu, Pacific Ocean 43 J6
Vilnius Lithuania 28 G6
Virgin Islands *U.K./U.S.A. territories* Caribbean Sea 15 O7
Virginia *State* U.S.A. 13 N6
Viscount Melville Sound Canada 10 H3
Vistula R. Poland 27 N2

Vladivostok Russian Federation 33 K8
Volga R. Russian Federation 29 J7
Vostok *Research station* Antarctica 9 N7

W

Wadi ar Rimah Saudi Arabia 31 J6
Wadi el Milk Sudan 19 J7
Wadi Masilah Yemen 31 L9
Wadi Ruaus Libya 18 H4
Wagga Wagga Australia 41 L8
Wake I. *U.S.A. territory* Pacific Ocean 43 J2
Wales *Region* U.K. 25 J4
Wallis & Futuna *French territory* Pacific Ocean 43 K6
Walvis Bay Namibia 20 G8
Warsaw Poland 27 N2
Washington *State* U.S.A. 12 F3
Washington D.C. U.S.A. 13 N6
Weser R. Germany 27 J2
West Siberian Plain Russian Federation 32 F5
West Virginia *State* U.S.A. 13 M6
Western Australia *State* Australia 40 E5
Western Ghats *Mountains* India 35 I7
Western Sahara *Disputed territory* Africa 18 D6
Western Samoa *Country* Pacific Ocean 43 L5
White Nile *River* Africa 19 K8
Whitney, Mt. U.S.A. 12 F6
Whyalla Australia 41 I7
Wilhelm, Mt. Papua New Guinea 42 H4
Wilkes Land *Region* Antarctica 9 M8
Windhoek Namibia 20 G7
Windward Passage *Strait* Cuba/Haiti 15 M7
Winnipeg Canada 11 J8
Winnipeg, L. Canada 11 I7
Wisconsin *State* U.S.A. 13 K4
Wollongong Australia 41 L8
Wrangel I. Russian Federation 8 E4 & 33 O4
Wrocław Poland 27 M3
Wuhan China 37 K6
Wyndham Australia 40 G3
Wyoming *State* U.S.A. 12 H4

X

Xi'an China 37 J6
Xingu R. Brazil 17 M4

Y

Yakutsk Russian Federation 33 K5
Yamal Peninsula Russian Federation 32 E4
Yamoussoukro Côte d'Ivoire 18 E8
Yangtze R. China 36 G6 & 37 K6
Yaoundé Cameroon 18 H9
Yaren Nauru, Pacific Ocean 43 J4
Yekaterinburg Russian Federation 32 E6
Yellow R. China 36 H5 & 37 K5
Yellowknife Canada 10 H5
Yemen *Country* Asia 31 L9
Yenisey R. Russian Federation 32 G4
Yerevan Armenia 31 K2
Yokohama Japan 37 O5
York, Cape Australia 41 K1
Yucatán Channel Cuba/Mexico 15 J6
Yucatán Peninsula Mexico 15 J7
Yugoslavia *Country* Europe 28 F8
Yukon R. Canada/U.S.A. 10 E6 & 12 D6
Yukon Territory *Province* Canada 10 E5
Yuzhno-Sakhalinsk Russian Federation 33 L7

Z

Zagreb Croatia 28 F8
Zagros Mountains Iran 31 L4
Zaire *Country* Africa 20 G3
Zambezi R. Africa 21 J6
Zambia *Country* Africa 21 I6
Zamboanga Philippines 39 K6
Zanzibar I. Tanzania 21 K4
Zaragoza Spain 25 K8
Zhengzhou China 37 J5
Zimbabwe *Country* Africa 21 I7
Zurich Switzerland 27 J5

GLOSSARY

Basin A dip, or depression, in the Earth's surface.

Bay A curve in the coastline.

Channel A wide stretch of water linking two areas of sea.

Climate The usual weather of an area.

Coastline The edge of the land, where it meets the sea.

Cold desert A place with low temperatures and very little rain.

Coniferous tree A type of tree that has leaves shaped like needles, such as a pine.

Continent A vast landmass. The seven continents are Africa, Antarctica, Asia, Australia, Europe, North America, and South America.

Coral Tiny sea animals that make chalky skeletons around their bodies. Over time, these skeletons pile up to form a reef.

Current A stream of water that flows through the sea.

Delta A buildup of sand, mud, and stones around a river where it enters the sea. A delta may form inland if a river cannot reach the coast.

Drought A long period of time when there is little or no rain.

Dune Sand that the wind has blown into a large mound.

Earthquake A sudden and often violent movement of the Earth's surface.

Equator An imaginary line that runs all the way around the middle of the Earth.

Erosion The gradual wearing away of the land, usually by wind or water.

Fault A large crack in the Earth's surface, or crust, caused by movement under the ground.

Fjord A steep-sided, coastal valley that has been created by ice and flooded by the sea.

Flash flood A sudden, spectacular flood that happens after a very heavy rainstorm.

Geyser A jet of hot water that spurts up from under the ground.

Glacier A huge mass of ice.

Gorge A steep-sided valley that has been created by a river. Deep gorges are called canyons.

Gulf A large, deep bay.

Hot desert A place with high daytime temperatures and very little rain.

Hurricane A storm that begins over oceans in tropical areas. Hurricanes are also known as cyclones.

Isthmus A narrow strip of land between two seas.

Landmass A large area of land surrounded by oceans.

Lava Hot, melted rock.

Mainland The main part of a landmass.

Mountain A place on the Earth's surface that is much higher than a hill.

Oasis A place in the desert where water reaches the surface.

Ocean An enormous body of salty water that is much bigger and deeper than a sea.

Peat bog A wetland where the ground is mostly made up of tightly packed, dead plants.

Peninsula An area of land that juts out into the sea.

Plain A large area of fairly flat land.

Plateau A large, raised area of flat land.

Polar zones The two vast cold regions of the Earth that lie north of the Arctic Circle and south of the Antarctic Circle.

Range A group of hills or mountains.

Rift valley A valley that has formed where the land has fallen down between two faults.

Season A time of year that has a special type of climate, such as winter.

Spit A long, narrow strip of sand and stones that reaches out from the land into the sea.

Stack A tall pillar of rock that stands in coastal waters.

State A part of a country. The United States is made up of 50 states. Australia has six states and two territories. Canada is made up of 12 parts that are known as provinces.

Strait A narrow stretch of water that connects two seas.

Temperate forest Tree-covered areas in the temperate zones. In places where the climate is very wet, temperate rain forests may grow.

Temperate grassland Grass-covered areas in the temperate zones, such as the prairies in North America and the steppes in Asia.

Temperate zones The two huge regions of the Earth that lie between the tropical zone and the polar zones.

Territory An area of land, or a town, that belongs to a country.

Tide The rise and fall of the sea, caused by the pull of the sun and moon on the water.

Trench A place on the ocean floor where two sections of the Earth's surface meet.

Tropical forest Tree-covered areas in the tropical zone. In places where the climate is very wet, tropical rain forests may grow.

Tropical grassland Grass-covered areas, with scattered trees in the tropical zone. They are also known as savanna.

Tropical zone The hot region of the Earth that lies between the Tropic of Cancer and the Tropic of Capricorn.

Tundra Cold, treeless lands that are mainly found near the ice-covered areas of the Earth.

Typhoon A small, violent storm that often forms in the Pacific Ocean.

Volcano The place where hot, liquid rock breaks through the Earth's crust.

Wadi A dry river valley in a desert. Usually a wadi will only carry water after a flash flood.

Wetland Places such as bogs and marshes where water lies on the surface of the land.

Whirlpool A strong, swirling movement in water. It is found at the bottom of a waterfall or where sea currents meet.

Acknowledgments

Geographical Advice:
Andrew Heritage & Roger Bullen
Dr. David R. Green
Illustrations:
Simone End & David Wright
Editorial Assistance:
Margaret Hynes
Design Assistance: Rhonda Fisher
Digital Base Map Production:
Professor Jan-Peter A.L. Muller,
Department of Photogrammetry &
Surveying, University College, London

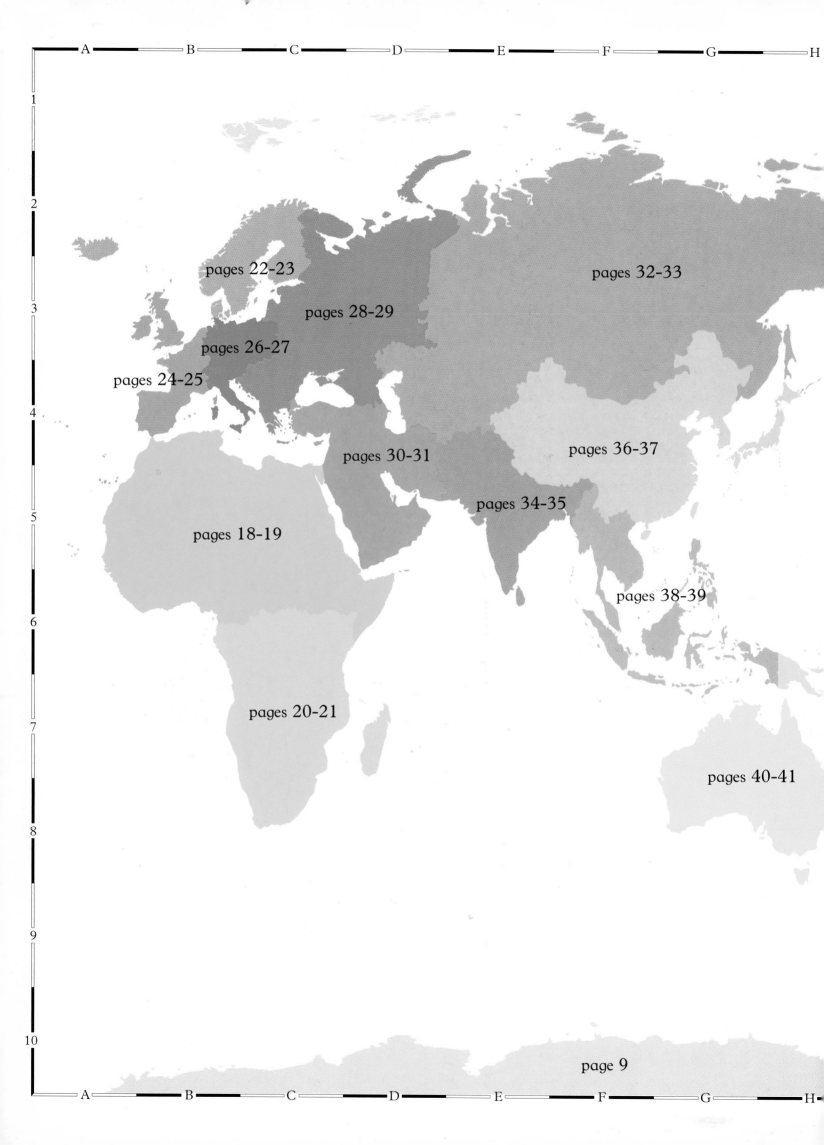